NATASCIA SERVINI, DAVID SHANKS, LUMA HAMEED & JULIEN VIOLETTE

SECONDARY LANGUAGES IN ACTION

IN ACTION SERIES

A **WALKTHRUs** PRODUCTION

Together we unlock every learner's unique potential

At Hachette Learning (formerly Hodder Education), there's one thing we're certain about. No two students learn the same way. That's why our approach to teaching begins by recognising the needs of individuals first.

Our mission is to allow every learner to fulfil their unique potential by empowering those who teach them. From our expert teaching and learning resources to our digital educational tools that make learning easier and more accessible for all, we provide solutions designed to maximise the impact of learning for every teacher, parent and student.

Aligned to our parent company, Hachette Livre, founded in 1826, we pride ourselves on being a learning solutions provider with a global footprint.

www.hachettelearning.com

Although every effort has been made to ensure that website addresses are correct at time of going to press, Hachette Learning cannot be held responsible for the content of any website mentioned in this book. It is sometimes possible to find a relocated web page by typing in the address of the home page for a website in the URL window of your browser.

Hachette UK's policy is to use papers that are natural, renewable and recyclable products and made from wood grown in well-managed forests and other controlled sources. The logging and manufacturing processes are expected to conform to the environmental regulations of the country of origin.

To order, please visit www.HachetteLearning.com or contact Customer Service at education@hachette.co.uk / +44 (0)1235 827827.

ISBN: 978 1 9152 6189 2

© Natascia Servini, David Shanks, Luma Hameed, Julien Violette 2025

First published in 2025 by
Hachette Learning,
An Hachette UK Company
Carmelite House
50 Victoria Embankment
London EC4Y 0DZ
www.HachetteLearning.com

The authorised representative in the EEA is Hachette Ireland, 8 Castlecourt Centre, Dublin 15, D15 XTP3, Ireland (email: info@hbgi.ie)

Impression number   10 9 8 7 6 5 4 3 2 1
Year   2029 2028 2027 2026 2025

All rights reserved. Apart from any use permitted under UK copyright law, no part of this publication may be reproduced or transmitted in any form or by any means, electronic or mechanical, including photocopying and recording, or held within any information storage and retrieval system, without permission in writing from the publisher or under licence from the Copyright Licensing Agency Limited. Further details of such licences (for reprographic reproduction) may be obtained from the Copyright Licensing Agency Limited, www.cla.co.uk

Typeset in the UK.
Printed in the UK.

A catalogue record for this title is available from the British Library.

CONTENTS

About the authors v

Introduction vii

Chapter 1 Debates and perspectives 1

What is languages teaching? 1

Why teach languages? 3

Communication versus accuracy 3

Approaches to teaching grammar 4

Use of target language 5

Decolonising the MFL curriculum 6

Chapter 2 Curriculum design principles 8

Backwards planning 8

Assessment 11

Primary-to-secondary transition 15

How to embed culture 18

Chapter 3 Inclusive teaching 20

Plan in incremental steps 21

Differentiation 22

Creating a non-threatening learning environment 25

100% participation 26

Equality, diversity and inclusion 27

Celebrating all languages 28

Collaboration 28

Chapter 4 Teaching new language _____ 30

Which language to teach _____ 30

Starter activities _____ 31

Introducing vocabulary _____ 31

Teaching phonics _____ 33

Teaching the skills _____ 36

Teaching listening _____ 39

Teaching speaking _____ 44

Teaching reading _____ 52

Teaching writing _____ 55

Teaching translation _____ 64

Teaching grammar _____ 66

Using digital technologies _____ 70

Chapter 5 Languages beyond the classroom _____ 78

Embedding hinterland in the curriculum _____ 78

Project-based learning _____ 79

Putting languages on the map _____ 96

Bibliography _____ 103

ABOUT THE AUTHORS

Natascia Servini is an assistant headteacher at a secondary school in east London and has been teaching French and Italian for 14 years. During her career, she has been a head of department and lead practitioner for languages across an academy trust. She also taught English as a foreign language for a year in Italy. In 2015 Natascia won the Association for Language Learning's Secondary Teacher of the Year award for her work in reviving languages in her inner London school, significantly increasing take-up of languages and improving outcomes at GCSE and A-level.

David Shanks has been teaching French in a range of inner-city contexts for the past 15 years. He works for Harris Federation, teaching French, supporting language departments and delivering training. Before completing his PGCE in French and EAL with the UCL Institute of Education, David taught in Norway and worked as a language assistant in France. His interests lie in assessment, creativity, use of technology, teacher development and the Association for Language Learning. His MA in education with King's College London included a dissertation on technology-facilitated oral homework, a summary of which was published in the 2021 Innovative Language Pedagogy Report.

Luma Hameed is an author of curriculum resources and the founder of *Yalla Arabi* online active books (www.arabicsawa.co.uk). She has delivered teacher training across a wide range of topics, nationally and internationally, and is a principal examiner at Cambridge University. Luma has a BEd, a PGCE and an MA in education: language, culture and identity. She taught Arabic and German at a secondary school in London and is passionate about promoting creative language learning and intercultural understanding. Luma is associate lecturer at Goldsmiths, University of London, and the leader of the Arabic Teachers' Council in London and Southern England.

Julien Violette is currently the lead languages consultant for a large multi-academy trust in London. He has been teaching languages since 2010. Before completing a PGCE at Goldsmiths, University of London, he studied translation at Charles de Gaulle University 3 in Lille, France. Julien has taught French and Spanish at secondary level across all key stages and German at KS3, and has led languages departments in two London comprehensive schools. His main areas of expertise are curriculum development, assessment and promoting languages studies. Other interests include long-term memory strategies, maximal use of target language by students and teachers, and effective questioning.

INTRODUCTION

If you talk to a man in a language he understands, that goes to his head. If you talk to him in his own language, that goes to his heart.

Nelson Mandela

This is the quote that every languages teacher knows. It's in classroom and MFL office displays, on presentation slides for European Day of Languages and careers events. It is what drives us as languages teachers. Being able to communicate in more than one language is a powerful tool: it allows us to live, work and love without borders. It builds relationships and understanding across cultures. Every languages teacher will have a story about how being a linguist has impacted positively on their life, from being able to study at a university in a different country, to meeting a romantic partner or lifelong friends; from having opportunities to get that dream job, to the satisfaction of being able to haggle in the souks of Marrakech, navigate the Paris metro or find the best pizza in Naples.

But being a languages teacher also comes with its challenges – from fighting for curriculum time to keeping the uptake at exam level high when numbers are declining nationally and, of course, responding to the question all language teachers will have heard at some point in their career: 'But everyone speaks English, so why do I need to learn another language?' It is for this reason that languages teachers are so keen to stress to what extent they contribute to an all-round education and are extremely committed to what they do. The languages teaching community thrives online and in person. Languages teachers plan school trips, competitions and spelling bees, decorate their classrooms with treasures they have collected on their travels, host foreign film lunchtime clubs ... The list goes on. We do it for the satisfaction of that moment when a student correctly uses a subjunctive for the first time in class or timidly asks for an ice cream in French on a day trip to Boulogne-sur-Mer and is delighted when they receive the correct item they ordered, making it all worth the effort.

With that in mind, we have aimed to write a book that speaks to the head and heart of languages teaching. We have covered teaching the different skills with advice for practical strategies that can be implemented straight away, as well as including sections on exciting project work and making the case for languages.

This book is written by and for languages teachers, taking into account the workload of marking those paragraphs about opinions on sports, conducting speaking assessments and planning all those wonderful extracurricular opportunities. In each chapter we have focused on implementation in the classroom with lots of low-prep, quick wins.

We have included a range of QR codes, weblinks and references to promote further engagement with the ideas we sketch here. A list of the links to the QR code resources is given here:

www.hachettelearning.com/john-catt/john-catt-extras

We hope that you can find inspiration to try something new, have a useful refresher of an activity you haven't included in your repertoire for a while or experiment and transform an idea into something new.

CHAPTER 1
DEBATES AND PERSPECTIVES

Dylan Wiliam's quote 'Everything works somewhere; nothing works everywhere' succinctly summarises why debates and varied pedagogical perspectives exist, and will persist, within languages teaching (Wiliam, 2018). Each teacher will have their own valid approach and perspectives, influenced by how they learned and were taught themselves, their initial teacher training, departmental approaches, ongoing professional development, the subject community and, above all, seeing what works with their students in their classroom.

As such, we are in an era where teachers and language departments often trial, select and blend pedagogical methods to best suit their context, taking into account their own beliefs and experience, the profile of their students, the amount of curriculum time they have allocated and the take-up of languages in their school. There is no one-size-fits-all approach and many teachers choose to take elements of different approaches and adapt them.

Below are outlined some key debates that it is professionally healthy for secondary languages teachers to be aware of.

What is languages teaching?

In its essence, languages are made of words (vocabulary) and structures regulated by rules (grammar) to communicate ideas, opinions and facts. Vocabulary and grammar have often been interpreted as the main tools required to acquire a language, but one cannot forget culture and the importance of teaching skills to unlock the language in real-life interactions. In contemporary languages teaching, those skills have been defined as listening, reading, speaking and writing and, to the present day, they continue to form the main part of assessing languages proficiency in tests and public examinations around the world. For example, they are broadly divided as such in assessment material which follows the Common European Framework of Reference for Languages (CEFR). In real-life use, those skills are what allow interactions and, all too often, learners need to use them simultaneously, for instance, in a conversation, listening to an interlocutor and responding verbally, or in a written exchange, reading a text or email and producing a written response. All skills can also be used independently, for instance, listening to music, the radio or a podcast, speaking by leaving a voice note or reading a book for pleasure. As such, teaching comprehension and production skills forms a large part of the role of languages teachers in secondary education, as it is widely accepted that teaching just vocabulary and grammar is not enough for students to acquire a language.

In addition to this, since the start of the millennium, the vision has also widened to consider the place of phonics and culture as part of the equation. In the UK, government policies aim to transfer the successes of phonics teaching in L1 in early education to the context of learning a foreign language and, while pronunciation has always been an important element of communication, phonics is now seen as one of the methods for acquiring accurate pronunciation. We will use a popular analogy that considers languages teaching as a braided rope made of five intertwined thinner strings. Three represent vocabulary, grammar and phonics (or more generally pronunciation) as the core elements of knowledge needed for language learning. A fourth represents practice of the four skills, unlocking comprehension and communication. The fifth string represents culture, necessary to become aware and open to different customs, viewpoints and beliefs, and often providing realistic contexts for communication.

In language classrooms, expect to see teachers facilitating vocabulary, grammar and phonics acquisition through lots of modelling and practice, through engaging games in pairs or groups, as well as silent individual work. Languages teaching relies on the use of an array of media and sources, including texts in different registers and genres, of audios and videos, of visual stimuli and props to prompt the learner, of stories and anecdotes to raise awareness of similarities and differences between cultures and nations. Expect to hear odd choral drilling of foreign words spoken in sync, songs and popular tunes rewritten to make language learning memorable and promote the acquisition of specific vocabulary or grammar and many other tricks of the trade that creative languages teachers rely on to make languages enjoyable and to engage and support learners.

Why teach languages?

Languages learning can play a significant part in the wider school curriculum provision in delivering on the core ethos and values that we want to instil in our students. In an ever-changing, global, yet complex and polarised modern world, languages learning raises awareness of different cultures, societies and ways of thinking, and provides the learner with the opportunity to understand and interact with them. Languages aim to 'foster pupils' curiosity and deepen their understanding of the world' (Department for Education, 2013), as well as to challenge stereotypes, prejudices and preconceptions. Knowing a foreign language is also very much functional: countless professionals from all fields who have studied a language have life stories about how their language skills have proved useful at work or led to promotion. Graduates in many subjects, including medicine and law, often report how languages have supported them in their studies. As such, our stand on the debate about whether languages studies should be compulsory or optional is that we believe all learners benefit from learning a language as part of their education as it helps them become well-rounded, open-minded, global citizens of the world.

Communication versus accuracy

Should our focus be on practical fluency and enabling students to communicate for real-world purposes or precise language use with correct grammar, vocabulary and pronunciation? At one end of this debate would sit a strong communicative language teaching approach, focusing on speaking and listening, target language ('TL) interaction, authentic tasks and role-plays. A benefit of this type of approach can be the positive impact on engagement and motivation by showing real-world relevance and allowing students to express themselves. A drawback can be the reduced emphasis on grammar, leading to gaps in even basic formal language knowledge and the ability to manipulate language. At the other end would be a traditional grammar–translation approach prioritising reading and writing, explicit grammar instruction and classes being conducted in learners' first language. This approach can build strong foundations and encourage clear, correct written language, but at the expense of speaking, listening, pronunciation, communication and potentially motivation. Sensibly, most teachers today take a balanced approach between communication and accuracy and adapt their focus according to the stage and needs of their learners as well as the requirements of qualifications and assessment.

Approaches to teaching grammar

There are two main approaches to teaching grammar in MFL classes: deductive and inductive. Each has its pros and cons. Some teachers prefer the deductive approach, especially for foundation-level students, as it provides direct, explicit grammar instruction, saving time and ensuring accuracy. This allows more time for practising other language skills and covering the syllabus within the restricted time offered at schools for MFL. Some students also enjoy this approach as they like exploring and memorising grammar rules.

Conversely, the inductive approach encourages students to identify patterns and deduce grammar rules on their own before practising the language which allows deeper understanding.

Given the diverse levels and abilities of students, a blended approach that combines both methods, integrates grammar and negotiation of meaning, and incorporates interactive, fun activities across all language skills is more effective (Conti, 2015). It is, however, important to consider the implications of cognitive load theory when planning grammar activities for your lesson.

Cognitive science research and languages

Recent years have seen a growth in research from the field of cognitive science influencing practice in schools. This has been facilitated by work and publications aiming to make such research more accessible to teachers and applicable to educational contexts, e.g. the ResearchEd movement, Rosenshine's 'Principles of instruction' (2012), the Deans for Impact's *The Science of Learning* (2015) and the Learning Scientists' 'Six strategies for effective learning' (2016). As a result, many teachers will be familiar with strategies from cognitive science such as:

- spaced learning (spreading learning over time with breaks in between)
- retrieval practice (encouraging active recall from memory through quizzes, questioning, and self-testing)
- managing cognitive load (recognising the limitations of working memory, considering the amount of mental effort required by a task and reducing unnecessary load)
- dual coding (combining verbal and visual information).

It is clear from the evidence base that cognitive science has the potential to improve learning and indeed many of the approaches have long been described as effective practice without the cognitive science label (spaced learning – revision lessons; retrieval practice – vocabulary tests; cognitive load – worked examples; dual coding – flashcards). Much can be leveraged from cognitive science research to support effective learning, but it is not in and of itself a silver bullet and a nuanced approach is needed. An over-mechanistic interpretation may neglect social, cultural and emotional considerations that are so inherent in our subject. The Education Endowment Fund's evidence review of cognitive science approaches in the classroom points to the fact that there are still gaps in the evidence base on how the principles can best be applied and this is more so the case when considering specific subjects. How cognitive science might be considered in languages will be covered in chapter 2.

Links: ResearchEd (https://researched.org.uk/)

Rosenshine's 'Principles of instruction' (https://eric.ed.gov/?id=EJ971753)

Deans for Impact, *The Science of Learning* (www.deansforimpact.org/tools-and-resources/the-science-of-learning)

The Learning Scientists, 'Six strategies for effective learning' (www.learningscientists.org/blog/2016/8/18-1)

Education Endowment Fund, 'Cognitive science approaches in the classroom' (https://educationendowmentfoundation.org.uk/education-evidence/evidence-reviews/cognitive-science-approaches-in-the-classroom)

Use of target language

A widely discussed topic of debate in languages learning is how the TL should be used in the classroom, and this has often fluctuated over decades, depending on what the most popular approach to languages learning was at the time. To understand why TL use in the classroom is subject to debate, we have to consider some common pros and cons of from the languages teaching community:

Pros of maximising TL use	Cons of maximising TL use
• Hearing the language in a context where learners may not otherwise get such opportunities outside the classroom. • Demonstrating genuine communicative use of the language.	• Confusing for learners if not understood, which can lead to demotivation and disengagement, accumulation of misconceptions, behavioural issues in the classroom. • Can appear to slow down the learning process, as teaching in the TL can take longer and require more checking for understanding.

It is also a more personal debate, as teachers will have their own stand on the subject, often influenced by beliefs, past learning experiences and current teaching experiences. We believe that there is no fixed, perfect percentage for TL use and that instead consideration should be given to the audience, the time and the place to use it or not. The aim should be an optimal use of the TL, striving to always use it whenever possible, while ensuring comprehension by tailoring it to the learners' level and the intended purpose. It should be carefully planned and structured so that it is accessible and assists the learning process without causing confusion and demotivation. It should be scaffolded and incremented in steps so it is progressively more demanding, but, most of all, it should be consistent and frequent, if learners are to engage with it. Classroom routines are an ideal opportunity to immerse learners into the TL, as they take place every lesson and, over time, they will become effortless. Greetings at the door or at your desk, taking registers, giving task instructions, praises, rewards and sanctions, all of these can be effectively implemented in the TL if done consistently and carefully planned so the same language is used or expected each time. In chapter 4 we will discuss further strategies for using the TL in the classroom (see 'Teaching listening', pp. 39–43, and 'Teaching speaking', pp. 44–52).

Link: for more on TL use in the classroom, see James Stubbs's blog (https://jamesstubbs.wordpress.com/)

Decolonising the MFL curriculum

Another recent area of debate has been how to decolonise and diversify our MFL curricula to make them inclusive and engaging for all. Decolonising the curriculum involves 'acknowledging and critically examining the influence of colonial legacies on education systems as a whole, and its various sub-components such as knowledge and the curriculum' (Johnson and Mouthaan, 2021) and diversifying the curriculum is 'expanding the curriculum to be inclusive and intersectional, including academics and readings from underrepresented backgrounds' (Teaching Matters blog). The Association for Language Learning has set up a working party to explore what this means for teachers of MFL, but there appears to be a consensus that our curricula should move from being (white) eurocentric to be inclusive of all countries where different languages are spoken (e.g. Hispanophere) and recognise the colonial past throughout our curriculum plans and not just during Black History Month or on International Francophonie Day. This also links with the multilingual approach. In an increasingly globalised and plurilingual world, the multilingual approach draws on students' heritage and prior language knowledge as an asset, making links between languages, increasing student motivation and outcomes.

Links: Johnson and Mouthaan, Runnymede 'Decolonising the curriculum: the importance of teacher training and development' (www.runnymedetrust.org/blog/decolonising-the-curriculum-the-importance-of-teacher-training-and-development)

Teaching Matters blog 'Mini-series: The importance of diversifying the curriculum: Reflections from the Senate Task Group' (https://blogs.ed.ac.uk/teaching-matters/mini-series-the-importance-of-diversifying-the-curriculum-reflections-from-the-senate-task-group/)

CHAPTER 2
CURRICULUM DESIGN PRINCIPLES

Designing an effective curriculum for language teaching and learning requires a nuanced balance of theory and practice to meet diverse learner needs and is crucial to secure high rates of student success. This chapter explores key principles and strategies that underpin successful curriculum design, starting with backwards planning to help set clear learning goals for different phases of learning so we can work towards them by creating a well-sequenced series of lessons and assessments. We delve into cognitive science, offering insights into structuring content to help students memorise key concepts and avoid overload and 'forgetting'. The chapter also examines the role of textbooks in selecting resources that align with curricular goals and learner outcomes. Finally, we address primary–secondary transition, highlighting strategies to ensure continuity and progression in language learning across key stages. Together, these elements provide a framework for creating a curriculum that inspires and empowers learners.

Backwards planning

Consider where you would like your students to be at the end of their language journey in your setting. A helpful exercise is to look through the specification of the end-of-school exam and make a list of the most essential skills, vocabulary and grammar required for students to achieve a top, middle and foundation grade. Once you have planned this out, identify which concepts students could master at each year and key stage point and when this will be revisited. Schemes of learning should also be looked at across years and key stages and not planned in isolation, so that links to prior learning can be made and concepts built upon over the years.

Another concept that can support you in identifying which concepts are the most important to focus on and revisit constantly is Gianfranco Conti's 'universals'. This is a similar concept to what is also referred to as 'core knowledge':

> The 'universals' are high surrender value grammar structures, lexical patterns and/or functions that you feel your students are currently not learning effectively due to insufficient exposure or practice in your extant input.

By making such language items your 'universals', you commit yourself to embed them systematically in your daily input, week in week out from the beginning to the end of the year.

Link: Gianfranco Conti, 'More on universals, desirables, controlled input and implicit learning' (https://gianfrancoconti.com/2017/10/21/more-on-universals-desirables-controlled-input-and-implicit-learning/)

Cognitive science

Although numbers vary, most research suggests that students will be able to hold around seven new items of vocabulary in their short-term memory per lesson. Therefore, once you have made your list of essential concepts, go back through the list and cut it down to its most critical concepts and give each of them time in your curriculum plan for students to embed them in their long-term memory. There is a temptation to move on quickly, to 'cover all the content', but if your students have not had sufficient time to master the foundations, then you will lose time later having to revisit them and progress will be hindered as they constantly have to go back and revise the foundation content. The aim is for foundation skills to be embedded in long-term memory so students can draw from their schemata and make connections to new learning.

Below are some languages-specific considerations for the cognitive science strategies referred to in chapter 1:

Strategy	Applications
Spaced learning	• Providing opportunities to revisit and recycle language across a curriculum, e.g. students in Year 7 might study a unit on personal description and adjectives. Then in a subsequent year revisit this topic to consolidate prior learning but extend to include an imperfect tense personal description with more complex and varied adjectives.
	• Recycling key high-frequency vocabulary across themes and topics, e.g. question words, conjunctions, intensifiers, opinion phrases, adverbs, time expressions.
	• Including elements of key prior learning on assessments, e.g. content from last topic/term/year.
	• Having students re-encounter and recycle key vocabulary, grammar or phonics through different skills and activity types within a lesson.

Strategy	Applications
Retrieval practice	• Including short, low-stakes quizzes as starter activities to recap last lesson (or prime students with recalling prior learning that will be relevant for the upcoming material). • Pitching for a high success rate. A whole class could get stuck with an L1 to L2 sentence translation with a more challenging word and lose motivation. Consider starting with multiple choice, true/false or L2 to L1 translation. Use early 'gimme' questions in the practice to engage all students and then gradually increase question challenge. • Considering open recall activities such as 'List all the vocabulary or phrases you can related to topic X.' • Introducing an element of time pressure (the length of a TL song?) to keep the practice snappy and not eat into lesson time for new learning. • Using the process to identify common misconceptions to address with the class.
Managing cognitive load	• Being aware of the limitations of short-term memory and considering how much new vocabulary, grammar and structures you are introducing per lesson. This will vary according to your learners, their prior learning, the complexity of the material and whether your goal is receptive or productive knowledge. • Providing sufficient input of language through the receptive skills before production. • Providing models and worked or 'explained out loud' examples, e.g. the three components and three stages of forming the perfect tense in French. • Chunking language together into short phrases or sentences facilitates communicative use and reduces the number of 'items' to remember. • Providing and then gradually removing scaffolding, e.g. models, vocabulary lists, sentence builders, sentence starters. • Avoiding extraneous material in resources – clear and logically presented language focusing on accessibility and the essential content.

Strategy	Applications
Dual coding	• Using gesture and expression when using the TL. • Using props and unambiguous images to introduce vocabulary or provide stimuli. • Using video to support listening comprehension. • Using graphical representations, e.g. for tense formations, tense timelines, mind maps.

When to use the textbook

Textbooks can be a fantastic resource to support teachers in their planning and often provide a useful framework for sequences of learning. As with all externally prepared resources, we should carefully consider how to maximise their use and adapt them according to the needs of our students. For example, when teaching a new grammatical concept, you may notice by the end of the lesson that your students still have many misconceptions, but the structure is not revisited until much later in the textbook.

When using textbooks to support your curriculum planning, you may wish to consider the following questions:

- What are my students interested in? What topics would they like to learn about?
- How can I make my lessons inclusive?
- How can I diversify and decolonise the curriculum?
- Which topics do students find difficult? How much time are we spending on them? How often do we revisit them? What order should I teach them in?
- Where can I include cultural knowledge and project work?
- Where do educational and international visits and enrichment fit?

Assessment

Assessment is crucial to inform our planning, but what forms can and should it take in a languages classroom and how often should we do it? The planning of assessment into our sequencing of learning is crucial. The traditional textbook-based model has neat modules of 5–6 weeks with a summative assessment, usually written, at the end, leaving teachers with up to 300 assessments to mark in the final 2 weeks of each half-term and then you move on to the new topic in the next half-term. This model also means we are using at least 6 hours per academic year on assessments. Is this the best use of learning time?

A current sequence of learning for key stage 3 using this model may look something like this:

Topic: Hobbies	
Week 1	Introducing hobbies with opinions and justifications *I like + hobby + because + it is + adjectives*
Week 2	Comparatives about hobbies *In my opinion + hobby + is + more/less + adjective + than + hobby*
Week 3	Talking about hobbies using the past tense
Week 4	Talking about hobbies using the future tense
Week 5	Revision and preparation for writing assessment
Week 6	Writing assessment marked by the teacher after the lesson *Write a paragraph giving your opinions on different hobbies, which hobbies you have done recently and what you would like to do in the future.*
Half-term	
Week 1	Listening and reading assessment self-/peer-marked

It is essential when we are planning assessment into our sequences of learning that we must above all consider the purpose.

> *If the purpose of robust curriculum planning is to ensure that pupils are taught the demanding aspects of a topic, then checking whether they have got it needs to be done through assessment [...] The critical thing is that it provides information about where the gaps are and also what can be celebrated, in terms of the distance travelled – so that we and our pupils are able to say we didn't know that before and now we do. And there is still this to be grappled with and understood.*
>
> (Myatt, n.d.)

Using these principles as our guide, how can we rethink assessment in MFL to support teacher workload, capture student progress and inform the next stages of our teaching?

- Using do now/starter activities as mini-assessments, but not vocab tests. During the first 10 minutes of the lesson, students could complete mini-translation tests, unjumble sentences or word snakes or complete multiple-choice questions to check understanding of prior content. Students can then peer-assess these.
- Live marking – once you have been able to establish routines and set well-scaffolded written tasks where students can work independently, circulate the classroom and give students individual live verbal or written feedback that they act upon immediately.
- Use whole-class feedback sheets rather than individual feedback in every student's book. You can access an example through the QR code.

- Plan speaking assessments and give students immediate feedback and record their marks. You will need to carefully plan independent learning for other students to allow you to do this.
- Consider the impact that assessment can have on learners' wellbeing, enjoyment of your subject and creating an environment where learners are welcome to make mistakes and these are celebrated as part of the learning process. How much lesson time is allocated to learning versus being assessed on the learning?
- How much feedback do learners need? Does the current amount of assessment planned provide too much or too little?

An alternative sequence of learning could look like this:

Topic: Hobbies	
Week 1	Introducing hobbies with opinions and justifications *I like + hobby + because + it is + adjectives*
Week 2	Comparatives about hobbies *In my opinion + hobby + is + more/less + adjective + than + hobby*
Week 3	Translation mini-assessment as starter activity self-/peer-marked by students. Teacher circulates and notes down common misconceptions, models and reteaches where appropriate. Talking about hobbies using the past tense
Week 4	Talking about hobbies using the future tense
Week 5	Recap of using past and future tenses Extended writing live marked by teacher in class. Teacher notes common misconceptions. Students complete a structured self-assessment task at the end using a checklist of the success criteria.
Week 6	Whole-class feedback on common misconceptions following extended writing, closing the gaps and consolidating learning
Half-term	
Week 1	Introducing new topic following cycle of previous half-term alternating writing assessment with speaking

Another important consideration is the sequencing of your summative assessment. A useful exercise is to print all your assessment papers for all year groups and lay them out in order. When looking from one assessment to the next, consider the following questions:

- Is there an increase in the level of challenge or are we just testing knowledge of a new topic?
- Is there scope in each assessment for all students to achieve the top grades? How is challenge embedded from the start or are students capped at certain grades?
- How are the assessments adapted for native or heritage speakers?
- Do the assessments build on prior knowledge? Are key structures and vocabulary revisited so students have to go back and continually revise previous content or is it just forgotten?

- Are we testing students' memory or are there also opportunities for us to assess language skills, such as applying a grammatical rule in a new context?
- Are these assessments happening at the right time to capture student progress and inform planning of next steps?
- Does the timing of the assessments support teacher workload?

Primary-to-secondary transition

To plan an effective curriculum, it is important to establish learners' starting points and be aware of prior learning. This can present particular challenges in secondary language teaching as the language(s) studied, time allocated, progress made and language learning experience in primary school can vary greatly from school to school. Furthermore, some secondary schools take students from many feeder primary schools, which can potentially lead to complete beginners and those with four years of strong languages teaching under their belt being in the same class – a clear challenge for delivering a suitable curriculum. Starting from scratch for everyone is a tempting solution but this does nothing to build upon prior learning, and the negative motivational impact of, for example, teaching the numbers one to ten to a student in their fifth year of learning a language is obvious. Despite these structural challenges, there are strategies and resources that can inform and facilitate transition from primary to secondary in languages.

Get informed on your primary feeder schools' offer

If your school has a single feeder school or is an all-through primary and secondary, this will be straightforward and present an excellent opportunity for planning a joined-up primary through secondary languages curriculum. However, in contexts with multiple feeder schools, a simple first step is to source a list of these schools from a member of senior leadership or a staff member in your school who oversees primary transition. Once you have the list, access each school's website to get an overview of the language(s) they teach, their allocated curriculum time and any curriculum documentation or schemes of work. Use this to inform your curriculum planning.

Ask the students/parents

Surveying students and/or parents directly can provide rich information to inform your curriculum and help teachers adapt their delivery. This is ideally done before students begin secondary school and could be completed during a parents' evening for incoming students, posted or sent via a digital form. An example survey and a student primary languages profile generated from the information obtained are shown below. Such profiles help teachers to build upon any prior knowledge or home language(s) and provide suitable support or challenge. If your school offers multiple languages, this is also an opportunity for students to select which language(s) they would like to study, which could have an onward positive impact on motivation for the subject.

Examples of an MFL KS2–KS3 transition questionnaire, tracker, mail merge and learner profile are accessible through the QR code.

Consider baseline tests or open-ended activities

Though there are debates around their validity and usefulness, baseline tests or language aptitude tests can give insights into students' prior language learning and potential. Be aware that they will not account for motivation, which is a key determiner of success in language learning. Where they might be most useful is if you have a good knowledge of (or input to) the students' primary school curriculum and want to get a sense of what they remember or their ability to analyse language and spot patterns. If your context could benefit from using them, it would be sensible to keep them short, attainable, low-stakes and non-threatening and use them to inform the teacher, as opposed to ability setting early in secondary. This could be achieved by using a language that students have not studied or by offering open-ended activities (e.g. 'Write any words or sentences you know in Spanish').

Consider differentiation within your curriculum

The options available for grouping students in languages will depend heavily upon a school's context, policy around setting, streaming and timetable constraints. Practice and preferences for ability or mixed groupings vary. Where the starting points of students in a class or between groups varies, it can be beneficial to decide in advance what is the 'essential' learning you want all students to master and then identify the more challenging language and concepts you want to use to 'stretch' individual learners or groups who are progressing more quickly. An example of 'essential' and 'stretch' learning can be accessed through the QR code.

Develop partnerships with your primary schools

This is valuable work that can have a significant impact on student progress longer term. Reaching out to, visiting and hosting primary colleagues to swap curricula, resources and ideally co-plan a primary-to-secondary curriculum allows for a better mutual understanding of contexts and can lead to smoother transition and better sequenced learning. For secondary teachers, developing an awareness of the first-language grammar taught and terminology used in primary can be leveraged in the secondary languages classroom. It can also be insightful to look at sample student work and visit lessons. This can serve as a powerful reminder for secondary teachers of what can be achieved in primary and of the need to create a secondary curriculum of sufficient challenge that builds upon learning and does not dumb down languages learning at secondary level. An example of work by a Year 5 student can be accessed through the QR code.

Links: the following links offer further resources to support the primary-to-secondary transition:

Research in Primary Languages: 'Primary Languages Policy in England – The Way Forward White Paper Report' (www.ripl.uk/wp-content/uploads/2019/02/RIPL-White-Paper-Primary-Languages-Policy-in-England.pdf)

Association of School and College Leaders: Transition Toolkits for:

- French (www.ascl.org.uk/ASCL/media/ASCL/Help%20and%20advice/KS2-KS3-French-Transition-Toolkit.pdf)
- Spanish (www.ascl.org.uk/ASCL/media/ASCL/Help%20and%20advice/KS2-KS3-Spanish-Transition-Toolkit.pdf)
- German (www.ascl.org.uk/ASCL/media/ASCL/Help%20and%20advice/KS2-KS3-German-Transition-Toolkit.pdf)
- Chinese (www.ascl.org.uk/ASCL/media/ASCL/Help%20and%20advice/Primary/KS2-KS3-Chinese-Transition-Toolkit.pdf)

Association for Language Learning: 'KS2-3 Transition Toolkit' (https://allconnectblog.wordpress.com/2016/01/05/all-connect-ks2-3-transition-toolkit/)

Association for Language Learning: 'Progression & Transition Wiki' (http://all-progressiontransition.wikidot.com/)

How to embed culture

With increased globalisation, migration and immigration, there is a growing need for an intercultural focus in the MFL class that enables students to better understand and respect other cultures and their own, and to participate effectively in a global world. Our students should be able to:

1. use their newly acquired language skills in a variety of real-life contexts crossing different cultures where the MFL is spoken
2. create personal connections with their own culture
3. encourage meaning-making where 'people are actively engaged in making sense of the situation – the frame, objects, relationships – drawing on their history of similar situations and on available cultural resources' (Zittoun and Brinkmann, 2012)

With this acquisition, students will develop richer plurilingual and pluricultural identities.

Hence, in the MFL curriculum, all themes and topics must be studied in a context that reflects the culture of countries where the MFL is spoken as well as the culture of students' home country. For practical ideas to embed culture in lessons, you can consider:

- **displays** – expose students to different cultural photos that help them visualise how real life is in the countries where the MFL is spoken. This can include maps, famous personalities, food, celebrations, tourist attractions and a special board with updated weekly news headlines from different countries relevant to particular topics.

- **celebrations** – share videos on special celebration days and festivals from different countries and allow students to compare them with a celebration they know, or celebrate the event by wearing similar costumes, learning expressions people say on that day, designing a card and preparing similar food. This can be shared with a linking school, if available, when celebrating a national day of languages or on the school's social media.

- **mini-library** – create a corner in your classroom with TL books, newspapers, magazines, board games and let students borrow them or allow a day once a month/term for reading them.

- **authentic materials** – at the end of each theme, expose students to authentic materials related to the same topic you are teaching. This includes proverbs, literary texts, visual art, calligraphy, graffiti, songs, dances and videos that reflect the lifestyles, cultural differences and values in different countries where the MFL is spoken.

- **project-based learning (PBL)** – engage students with various real-life cultural topics and meaningful TL use, ensure to connect the topic with students' personal culture and ask them to reflect on it or compare it with their personal life, and encourage them to work on a creative project (see chapter 5 for a practical example) and share it with the class or a wider audience.

CHAPTER 3
INCLUSIVE TEACHING

Every student and every class are unique. This is one of the joys and privileges of teaching, although it presents an obvious challenge: how best to design and teach a curriculum to account for the diverse strengths, needs, interests, backgrounds and experiences of all students. A non-exhaustive list of the ways in which students differ that could influence their language learning is:

- age
- gender
- prior attainment/ability
- prior language learning experience
- motivation and perceptions of languages
- working memory
- personality, resilience and self-efficacy
- bilingualism, any home language(s) or additional language(s) being learned inside or outside school
- English as an additional language (EAL)
- peer and family perceptions of language learning
- prior exposure to others' languages and cultures, e.g. through travel or opportunities to develop cultural capital
- socioeconomic status
- outside interests and future aspirations
- special educational needs and disabilities (SEND)
- safeguarding concerns

That each of these factors can influence different students in different ways demonstrates the complex and rich tapestry in each classroom. As such, building relationships and a good understanding of each individual student's strengths and needs over time is perhaps the most important and effective work a teacher can undertake to support inclusive teaching. Making use of student data, EAL registers, SEND registers and profiles (which should include personalised teaching strategies), discussing approaches and planning with other staff (e.g. teachers, class tutor, pastoral lead, head of year, EAL coordinator, SEND coordinator) and communicating with parents are all ways to build up a picture of each student.

Monitoring and assessing student work give a window into the 'black box' of student thinking, progress and misconceptions and allow the teacher to give feedback and subsequently adapt their teaching. Paying close attention to students' comments, conversations, reactions and responses across the different skills (and in between activities) can also provide incredibly rich insights for the inclusive teacher. The minutiae and many interactions of every classroom can help identify areas of interest and opportunities to celebrate, as well as knowing when to move on, when to challenge, when to support or reteach and when follow-up outside of lesson may be necessary. Greeting students at the door of the classroom and quizzing them on their interests/opinions/weekend plans (in the TL or English as appropriate), initiating conversations at lunch/break time, using parents' evenings effectively and participating in extracurricular activities are all 'ways in' to better understand your students.

Along with knowing individual students, there are a number of broader strategies and approaches teachers and departments can use to support outcomes, high aspirations and a sense of success and belonging for all.

Plan in incremental steps

Plan step by step in the short term and take into account the limitations of working memory to increase accessibility and confidence. For example, in any given lesson or unit of lessons, do not overload students with too much new vocabulary and/or new grammar all at once. Instead, plan a coherent sequence of linked activities that first present and input language, before providing opportunities to practise and finally inviting production. In the medium and longer term, plan for students to have ample opportunities to practise, revisit and transfer vocabulary and grammar. For example, early in their secondary course, students may learn how to describe their physical appearance and personality in the present tense using the key irregular verbs 'to be' and 'to have'. This topic might then be revisited later at greater depth and complexity by including the imperfect tense to describe 'what I used to be like when I was younger' and using a range of more complicated adjectives. This 'spiral curriculum' approach balances the need to revisit content to interrupt forgetting, providing a sense of familiarity and support at the same time as progress and challenge.

Differentiation

Inclusive classrooms tailor instruction to fit the needs and current level of different students. This is often referred to as 'differentiation' and more recently as 'adaptive teaching'. The overarching goal is to keep learning simultaneously accessible and suitably challenging for each student while maintaining a cohesive lesson and not lowering expectations or leaving some students behind. This requires pre-planning as well as in-lesson formative assessment that monitors and then adapts to how learning unfolds. This complicated balancing act is something of an art and is ideally embedded throughout all aspects of planning and lesson delivery. How the main modes of differentiation might manifest themselves in the languages classroom are listed below.

Differentiation by task

Different tasks are set for students according to their ability and needs. This has the advantage of pitching the work at a suitable level but can potentially cap expectations. It can also create challenges in managing the classroom environment as students are completing different work, making giving instructions and feedback more challenging. There are times when separate tasks are necessary (e.g. in preparing for tiered exam question practice), although preparing varied tasks has an obvious impact upon teacher planning workload. Some ways of overcoming this tension without creating a multitude of different worksheets every lesson can include:

- Adapting the complexity of the teacher's oral questioning between students. Compare: Do you like football? Do you like football or tennis? What sport do you like? What sport do you like and why? What sport did you like when you were younger and why? What sport would you like to try and why?
- Increasing or reducing the pace at which a task is to be completed and setting additional in-task challenges or extension tasks (see 'Early finishers' below).
- Varying the task depth from the same source material, e.g. in a listening comprehension all students are required to indicate each person's favourite food. This could easily be extended to invite more

able students to also provide additional information, transcribe or translate language.

Name	Favourite food

→

Name	Favourite food	Reason / Additional info / Transcription / Translation

- Adapting the level of support. The same task completed with support or completely from memory is in itself a very different task in terms of cognitive challenge.

Differentiation by support

The level of challenge is varied by the degree of support that students receive when completing a task. The support could take various forms:

- direct 1:1 or small-group support from the teacher or teaching assistant
- giving the option to work with a partner or in a group
- permitting access to reference materials, such as exercise books, vocabulary lists, knowledge organisers or a sentence builder
- task-specific language support, e.g. glossing on a reading text or providing the words to be inserted in a gap-fill exercise; this can be easily added to or removed from a whole-class resource beneath a dotted line
- providing scaffolding through writing frames, sentence starters, structure strips or giving the first letter of a word
- providing example sentences or model paragraphs

A sample dotted-line support resource can be accessed through the QR code.

Differentiation by outcome

The same more open task is set for all students, who complete it to the best of their ability. This is most obvious in writing and speaking, where student responses can vary in length, accuracy and complexity. The teacher can still usefully guide students by providing success criteria, e.g. indicating the length, language and grammar that would be expected in a standard/middle/top-grade response.

Early finishers

For early finishers, perhaps more able students or native speakers, it is useful to plan extension activities that will challenge and stretch. These could come from a pre-prepared bank of resources, cultural articles, TL books or magazines, or reading or grammar exercises from a more advanced textbook. However, it does not always need to be onerous for the teacher in terms of preparation. For example, imagine a more able student has just completed writing a paragraph describing their daily school routine and is waiting for classmates to finish. The teacher could verbally and quickly set a range of stretch tasks, such as:

- Highlight all your reflexive verbs/opinions/time phrases.
- Write about your weekend routine.
- Include three things that you do not usually do and why.
- Can you now include five of our higher-level language phrases from the wall/grammar point X or two idiomatic phrases?
- Write about what you did yesterday or will do tomorrow.
- Imagine you are celebrity/historical figure X. Write a daily routine from their perspective.
- Write about a friend/family member's daily routine in the third person.
- Can you turn to the back of your book and now write from memory, without any support resources?
- Assess your paragraph against these marking criteria. What score would you give your response and why?

The bigger picture and student independence

An opening step for lessons that supports all students is outlining the objectives, purpose of the learning and where it fits into the bigger picture. For example:

> Today we're learning vocabulary for film genres and adjectives to describe films. We'll build upon the basic opinion phrases we learned last year, so that at the end of this half-term we can write a film review of our favourite films for our penpal letters.

If students are clearer on what they are doing, why and why now, this can improve engagement and so free up the teacher to direct their attention to those who might need additional support.

Encouraging greater classroom independence can empower students and release the teacher to support those who are encountering barriers. 'Three Bs before me' is a neat strategy for training students to be more independent and exhaust simple avenues of support. Before asking the teacher a question, students are encouraged to go through these three steps:

1 **Brain** – have you thought carefully about your question? Have you thought of what you have already learned and checked instructions?
2 **Browse** – have you browsed available resources, e.g. your book, the board, reference materials such as a textbook, vocabulary list, sentence builder or dictionary?
3 **Buddy** – have you checked with a classmate? Is the person beside you working through the task and able to explain?

This encourages autonomy and can significantly reduce the amount of unnecessary or already-answered questions – especially relevant in the languages classroom where the teacher can otherwise be inundated with 'How do you say X?' questions.

Creating a non-threatening learning environment

The languages classroom can be an intimidating and anxiety-inducing place for some students and this can have a knock-on negative impact upon progress and motivation. The teacher can do a lot to combat this by creating a supportive, collaborative environment and instilling a 'have a go' atmosphere. Teaching students that everyone can expect to make mistakes and sharing yours from the course of your language learning journey can help demonstrate that this is just part and parcel of the language learning process. Consider how to sensitively and judiciously correct students, especially when speaking the TL. This might involve correcting the main error and ignoring others, signposting support materials or bouncing to peers for help, before returning to the student to allow them to finish an interaction with success and praise from the teacher. The teacher's choice of language around errors can also support a positive classroom culture. For example, instead of directly correcting a student who says *'j'ai allé'* for the first time with the correct *'je suis allé'*, the teacher might instead opt for something along the lines: 'Almost there, I see you've made an intelligent mistake and it's one others will have made too. Who can help? What should we say instead? And who can explain why *j'ai allé* is a logical mistake?'

100% participation

Participation and thinking lead to learning. If students are able to opt out of engaging with the work at hand, they will struggle to learn and remember. This can quickly lead to knowledge gaps that affect future learning, lead to task abandonment or a drop in motivation. Using the traditional 'hands up' to question a class means mainly the more able and confident students (who, on balance, have the right answer because their hand is up!) dominate the environment. This means some students can be hidden by the more confident and by the classroom practice, often inadvertently excluding them from learning and high expectations for all. There are several ways around this problem, for example:

- No 'hands up' or 'cold calling' where there is a culture that the teacher may call on any student at any time to answer (while remaining sensitive to any specific needs or anxieties).
- Increase wait time after questions to allow all students sufficient time to think. The 'think-pair-share' structure allows students to prepare individually and with a partner before responding to the teacher in front of the whole class.
- Using whole-class response systems such as mini-whiteboards or voting, e.g. 'On the count of 3, vote with your fingers, is the answer 1, 2, 3 or 4?')
- Increasing the ratio of individual/paired activities to those that are conducted through the teacher, e.g. rather than the teacher orally quizzing the class on the meaning of a set of 10 phrases, students do this in pairs or individually. This has a powerful multiplication effect. With everything funnelled through the teacher, only 10 questions will be asked and answered. However, paired quizzing in a class of 30 boosts this to potentially 150 (15 × 10) questions asked and answered, increasing student thinking and participation significantly.

Balance variety with routines

A variety of task types across and mixing the skills can help keep lessons engaging and of interest to students. However, it is important not to confuse engagement with entertainment. The use of games and competition within activities only works if they support learning and do not cause unnecessary distraction. Structure and routines benefit all students as well as particularly those with SEND or EAL. Expectations become clear through repetition and familiarity, meaning less time is spent on the mechanics of how to complete an exercise and more time thinking about and engaging with language. It is useful to have a core toolkit of activity types that are effective and familiar to students to draw upon across different themes, topics and grammar points.

Equality, diversity and inclusion

It is important and healthy to reflect regularly upon the curriculum and lessons through the lens of equality, diversity and inclusion (EDI). Do the topics taught and materials used represent your classroom? Are students exposed to a diverse range of representations and cultures from around the TL world or are stereotypes and eurocentricity reinforced? Are opportunities taken to let students learn about different perspectives and some of the uncomfortable truths behind the complex history of languages? Do students learn about race, religion, women's and LGBTQ+ rights? If the answer is 'not yet', Edexcel's series 'Permission to Speak: Amplifying Marginalised Voices Through Languages' and the Association for Language Learning's 'Decolonise MFL Curriculum Special Interest Groups' are excellent starting points for ideas and inspiration.

Links: 'Permission to Speak: Amplifying Marginalised Voices Through Languages' (www.pearson.com/en-gb/schools/subject-resources/modern-languages/why-languages-matter/diversity-and-inclusion/permission-to-speak.html)

Decolonise MFL Curriculum Special Interest Groups (www.all-languages.org.uk/about/community/special-interest-groups/de-colonising-the-curriculum/)

Here are a few practical steps that could be considered to start addressing EDI in your MFL curriculum:

- Design a curriculum that supports students in exploring an MFL as a global language, rather than just as one spoken language in a specific country.
- Plan to create resources that allow learners to explore the cultures of different countries where the language is spoken.

- Challenge students' conscious or unconscious misconceptions about customs and traditions in countries which they may consider 'closed-minded', 'backward', 'living in the desert', etc.
- Expose students to images and stories of diverse people and places and allow them to create a personal connection.

Celebrating all languages

Many students possess rich and impressive skills in a range of languages, including perhaps the one being taught as part of the curriculum. As well as a need that requires teachers to provide suitably pitched and challenging work, this is something to celebrate and draw upon in the classroom. Native speakers can help model pronunciation or role-plays, be invited to share their knowledge and experiences, support peers or given a pen to circulate and live-mark with the teacher. Asking students to teach you words or phrases in their language can be a powerful leveller and a blank 'teach the teacher your language' exercise book at the front of class can lead to students staying behind after lessons to show off their language skills. As part of languages celebration events, such as the European Day of Languages, students can run taster sessions teaching their language. Encouraging and supporting students to gain accreditation in community languages help to show that all language skills are valued in the school and gaining a qualification can be of direct positive benefit to the student, as well as a source of pride.

Link: European Day of Languages (https://edl.ecml.at/)

Collaboration

Teaching is at its most inclusive when all school staff work collaboratively alongside parents to get the best out of each student, especially those with particular needs. Schools are often time-poor environments, so an extra parent phone call, trip to the SEND or EAL department or planning meeting with a learning support assistant can easily drop off the priority list. However, the effort is worthwhile; parents and specialist colleagues will have a deeper knowledge and understanding of the student compared with the average classroom teacher who interacts with larger groups the majority of the time. They can often impart practical strategies and golden nuggets of advice on how to get a student to fulfil their potential in the languages classroom.

Links: here are some further resources to support SEND in languages teaching:

David Wilson, 'Languages' (www.specialeducationalneeds.com/home/languages)

David Wilson, 'SEND, EAL, Gifted and Talented' (www.specialeducationalneeds.com/home/inclusion)

Inclusive Practice in Language Learning (www.incpill.com) hosts some of Hilary McColl's materials on language learning and inclusion from the former website 'Languages Without Limits'

Connor, J. (2017) *Addressing Special Educational Needs and Disability in the Curriculum: Modern Foreign Languages.* London: Routledge.

Bryfonski, L. and Mackey, A. (2023) *The Art and Science of Language Teaching.* Chapter 7 'How do I best support neurodiverse learners?'

CHAPTER 4
TEACHING NEW LANGUAGE

The input of new language is at the heart of languages teaching: what we choose to teach, when, how and for how long are crucial decisions we have to make as languages teachers to get the best from our students. Most current exam systems assess progress in language learning via the following skills: listening, reading, speaking and writing, including translation. This chapter examines each element in turn and suggests some practical approaches which we have found to be effective in engaging learners and helping them to progress.

Which language to teach

Research on teaching new language is ever evolving and has become the subject of much debate in recent years. However, it has become widely accepted that teaching language in 'chunks' rather than as individual items of vocabulary supports learners in being able to communicate more effectively, leading to increased motivation and progress.

An example lesson structure for a lesson of 50 min to 1 hour in which new language is being introduced using PPP (presentation, production and practice) could look like this:

1 starter activity – recapping previous learning that can also be applied to the lesson
2 introducing new vocabulary
3 games to practise new vocabulary
4 receptive activity (reading and/or listening) that practises new vocabulary
5 productive activity (speaking and/or writing) that practises new vocabulary
6 plenary – reviewing the learning

When planning these lessons, it is vital to ensure that the chunks of new vocabulary are continuously revisited in each activity as we know learners need to see and hear a new word around 10 times before they can start using it from memory. If you are using listening or reading activities from a textbook, you will need to make sure your key structures are covered and there are no 'curveballs' to distract learners or take the lesson in a different direction. For example, if you are teaching a lesson on food in French to beginners, you will need to decide if the 'chunk' is 'I like + noun' or 'I eat + partitive article + noun'.

In this chapter, we aim to provide guidance on lesson planning by breaking down the main components of language learning, as defined in previous chapters, in order to examine how each element can be taught. We suggest approaches that we have found effective in our classrooms.

Starter activities

A starter activity should be a quick, quiet, independent 10-minute activity that settles learners at the beginning of the lesson. This allows you as the teacher to complete the 'business' at the start of the lesson: register, catching up with any absent students, providing teaching assistants or foreign language assistants with resources etc. Starter activities are a fantastic opportunity to revisit previous learning, which helps with memory and retention as well as supporting independent learning. The activity should be self- or peer-assessed so you can move on quickly to the main task.

Effective starter activities include:

- multiple-choice quizzes
- mini-translation or vocab tests – remember to test in 'chunks' rather than individual items of vocabulary
- retrieval grids
- word snakes, unjumbling sentences, gap-fill – take care to differentiate these for students with SEND such as visual impairments or dyslexia

Link: Lightbulb Languages has a fantastic range of free resources to support planning starter activities (www.lightbulblanguages.co.uk/resources-starters-n-plenaries.htm)

Introducing vocabulary

When teaching new vocabulary we need to plan in activities for learners to see and hear the chunk multiple times. Choral repetition is still highly popular and effective in allowing learners to hear models of correct pronunciation and for them to practise in a low-stakes, safe environment.

31

A structure for choral repetition that increases in challenge could look like this:

1. Images that are linked to the chunks are shown on the board, the teacher says the phrase, checks meaning and the whole class repeats. Repeat this cycle several times.
2. Ensure the text is removed and only the image remains. Say one of the target chunks. Students use red or green cards, thumbs up or down or mini-whiteboards to indicate if the phrase you have said corresponds to the image.
3. Choral repetition of all the vocabulary again.
4. Point to an image and give two options, again using your whole-class Assessment for Learning (AfL) techniques or targeted questioning to elicit the correct response.
5. Choral repetition of all the vocabulary again.
6. Targeted questioning without prompting to see if learners can reproduce the vocabulary.
7. If learners are not able to confidently produce any items of vocabulary at this stage, start again. Do not be afraid to take up more lesson time, this is an essential part of the learning that needs to be mastered for learners to be successful later in the lesson.

Games to practise new vocabulary

There are a wealth of games that you can find online for practising vocabulary and supporting memory. Having a repertoire of five or so games and creating template slides for them, so that you can then adapt to fit the new vocabulary being taught, helps save a huge amount of time. We may think that learners would get bored with playing the same games, but, on the contrary, they enjoy the routines and consistency. Learning time is not wasted constantly explaining and modelling new activities and when done on rotation they are not repetitive.

Some easy-to-plan games that can be adapted to any topic are:

- Splat – two students race to touch the image that corresponds to the phrase. Reuse your choral repetition slide for this.
- Os and Xs
- Battleships
- Trapdoor
- One dice, one pen
- Sentence stealer and Mind-reader games from Gianfranco Conti

This is also where technology could be put to great use. Websites such as Memrise, Quizlet, Kahoot! and Blooket allow you to create your own games for free using your chosen 'chunks'. These can also be set for homework.

Teaching phonics

In recent years phonics has undergone a resurgence in popularity, initially in the acquisition and development of literacy in the learner's first language (L1) but also later in the context of second-language (L2) acquisition. Although research on the latter is relatively recent and sparse, the teaching of phonics in secondary education has started to be recognised by many as beneficial to the process of learning a second language.

Before looking further into this, it is important to distinguish between the teaching of phonics in L1 and in L2. Indeed, in L1, the learner has already acquired a lot of knowledge of the language orally and phonics is used as a method to teach the learner to decode written words and associate them with the familiar oral version they already know, allowing them to comprehend a written text. However, in L2 the learner usually does not have such prior knowledge of the language and, as a result, learning the sound, spelling and meaning of vocabulary often occurs simultaneously. Consequently, the explicit instruction of phonics in the teaching of a second language has so far been shown to have an inconclusive impact on the learner's comprehension skills (Woore et al., 2018). Nonetheless, other positive conclusions have been observed. For instance, the explicit instruction of phonics can allow the learner greater autonomy in decoding and associating sounds and spelling with greater accuracy when reading aloud (Hawkes, 2019). In addition, some studies have also concluded that such instruction may also have a positive impact on vocabulary acquisition (Woore et al., 2018).

In the UK the teaching of phonics in foreign languages learning, previously taught only at university level, was first acknowledged in the Teaching Schools Council's MFL pedagogy review of 2016, led by Ian Bauckham, and has since been embraced by the latest Ofsted Research Review Series (2021). This document defines phonics as one of three pillars of language learning, alongside vocabulary and grammar. As a result, a new GCSE examination has been developed that aims to assess the learner's knowledge of phonics in tasks such as dictation and read-aloud. In this section we will not debate this change, but, instead, we will examine how the explicit instruction of phonics and its integration in existing languages curriculum can be beneficial and how it may indeed allow the learner to read and pronounce the language more accurately than when sound system correspondence (SSC) is only implicit. Furthermore, research by Woore (2022) shows that phonics teaching certainly does not hinder the learning. Below we will discuss effective phonics teaching strategies that can easily be implemented in the classroom alongside any existing curriculum.

How to deliver phonics

The language curriculum is often already packed and, depending on the provision, it can be difficult to imagine adding more content to it. However, explicit phonics instruction can be as short as a segment of 10 minutes in the overall weekly lesson time. In that segment the teacher should offer explicit modelling of a specific sound, followed by practice to cement the new knowledge.

We recommend selecting sounds that may be particularly relevant to the vocabulary taught in the lesson to make this initial connection with the content and to provide learners the opportunity to accurately produce the new language orally. As such, it can be particularly beneficial to include phonics content in schemes of work and mid-term plans in order to map the most important and frequent sounds that the learner will be exposed to. SSC lists have been recently prescribed in the GCSE subject content (Department for Education, 2023) and useful examples of lists of the main sounds for French, Spanish and German can be found on the Language-Driven Pedagogy (LDP) resource portal (https://resources.ldpedagogy.org), which we recommend reviewing.

However, we also recommend that the practice should not exclusively take place with the vocabulary taught in a specific topic. Indeed, in order for learners to develop decoding skills and gain in confidence when pronouncing words in the TL, the practice should progress towards unfamiliar words that share the same sound, so learners can apply their new knowledge in new settings and progressively become more confident and autonomous in decoding new language.

In the modelling phase, the teacher can use strategies such as chorus drill (listen and repeat). Short discussions about the mouth placement, the combination of letters that may all share this sound and the distinction with another distinctive sound may also serve as effective modelling. Examples of such resources are accessible through the QR code.

Following the initial input, short practice activities in succession may allow for more meaningful and controlled practice. The practice should be multimodal, that is, allow learners to experience the sound through different media and skills. For instance, through listening and reading, activities such as spotting the odd-one-out, that is, the word that does not share the same sound. Also, circling the word you hear in a list of words that are close in spelling. Through listening and writing, learners can practise transcribing a syllable, a word or a sentence that they hear (dictation). Practice through reading and speaking could include reading a text aloud with a partner. Practice through speaking, listening and writing could be done using peer dictation. A variety of multimodal phonics practice activities and games can be found for public use on the LDP resource portal.

Outside of the explicit phonic segment, this instruction should be followed up in the rest of the lesson and the teacher should use questioning and live feedback to regularly revisit and assess the learners' knowledge of SSC. This can be particularly impactful in the teaching of grammar, when patterns are affected by differences in spelling and sound and therefore where listening practice can help cement the understanding of endings, their differences in sound and spelling.

CH	CA/CO/CU	CI/CE
chilo (key-lo)	**c**asa (ka-sa)	**ci**ao (ch-ow)
GLI	SCI/SCE	GN
lu**gli**o (loo-lyo)	**sci**are (she-are-eh)	**gn**occhi (gn-o-key)

For more on phonics teaching, we recommend Sue Cave and Jean Haig's work on 'physical French phonics', which combines sounds, gestures and images to teach key French sounds. Their work offers a wealth of engaging activities for practice and production and can be particularly successful in the early years of languages teaching (www.physicalfrenchphonics.co.uk).

Teaching the skills

Foreign languages curricula often focus on the acquisition of language through vocabulary and grammar and this is usually achieved by way of topics. However, assessments in foreign languages generally test learners' abilities in the following four skills, which can be categorised as: receptive skills (listening and reading) and productive skills (speaking and writing). Indeed, it is easy to understand why the majority of public examinations do assess learners' knowledge through these skills. England's national curriculum, published in September 2013, provides the following guidance for secondary languages curricula:

> The teaching should enable pupils to express their ideas and thoughts in another language and to understand and respond to its speakers, both in speech and in writing. It should also provide opportunities for them to communicate for practical purposes, learn new ways of thinking and read great literature in the original language. Language teaching should provide the foundation for learning further languages, equipping pupils to study and work in other countries […]

The national curriculum for languages aims to ensure that all pupils:

- understand and respond to spoken and written language from a variety of authentic sources
- speak with increasing confidence, fluency and spontaneity, finding ways of communicating what they want to say, including through discussion and asking questions, and continually improving the accuracy of their pronunciation and intonation
- can write at varying length, for different purposes and audiences, using the variety of grammatical structures that they have learnt
- discover and develop an appreciation of a range of writing in the language studied.

As such, it is equally important that the curriculum and the teaching focus a significant part of the practice on developing receptive and productive skills, which will allow learners to use their language skills outside the classroom, in a communicative context, and ultimately access assessment and public examinations. In this and subsequent sections, we discuss effective strategies for teaching the different skills.

Common misconceptions about language skills

A common mistake that teachers can make early in their career is to think that skills will be acquired through practice only and that the more they expose their learners to comprehension and production tasks, the better the learners will perform over time. However, without careful consideration and planning, simply practising those skills can lead to little or no progress and, in fact, may result in learners feeling demotivated and disengaged if they feel those tasks are too challenging. Classroom experience shows that a more meaningful practice of those skills comes from careful planning and scaffolding, so that learners are exposed to comprehension and production tasks when they have become confident with the language, that is, after it has been amply modelled in the acquisition phase.

This does not mean that listening, reading, speaking and writing must be absent from the acquisition phase of the new language. In fact, they are essential to it, but distinctions must be made in the practice of these skills as the learning sequence progresses.

Strategies for skill practice

At this stage it is important to distinguish between different types of practice, their purpose and how to vary them to better equip learners with strategies for comprehension (listening, reading) and production (speaking, writing). The first distinction is between the practice of language within the restriction of the new language, that is, practice within high comprehensible input, where at least 90% of the language in the task is already familiar to learners. Such practice is particularly effective in the early stage of language acquisition as it allows learners to practise the new language in the safety that their knowledge is enough to comprehend or produce the language.

Often, such tasks are also referred to as 'controlled input' (in listening and/or reading activities), where the source or text has been designed by the teacher to guarantee that it uses the new and familiar language almost exclusively, thus removing any potential barriers to comprehension. For production (speaking, writing), we refer to 'controlled output' practice, where again the language expected to be produced by learners is that which is taught in the lesson.

Controlled input and output tasks nearly always have a right and wrong answer, so that learners are supported in their learning and can identify what is correct and what is incorrect. Such practice should take place during the new language acquisition phase and repeated until learners become confident with the language. Once learners have successfully practised the language and gained in confidence, the teacher can offer more challenging comprehension and production practice, which could include unfamiliar elements as well as more open-ended outcomes.

In comprehension (listening, reading), such tasks may include sources or texts that use words which learners may not have seen before or which may have been learned in previous topics. This practice may also expose students to authentic sources and texts that have not been specifically designed for the purpose of teaching but provide a meaningful model of how the language can be used outside the classroom walls.

In production (speaking, writing), open-ended tasks provide learners with the opportunity to produce the language more freely and in conjunction with language they have previously acquired. These tasks may be more high-risk as learners are less restricted and thus may attempt to produce language outside of the scaffold they were given in earlier stages.

Learners will be able to access comprehension and open-ended production tasks only if they are confident and ready, so it is the role of the teacher to ensure that the transition from controlled practice to open practice is carefully planned and progress is continuously monitored.

In the following sections, we explore this methodology further for each of the distinct skills. Despite this division, it is, however, necessary to acknowledge that skills do not have to be systematically practised separately from one another and, in fact, multiskill practice should also be encouraged at various stages of learning. Indeed, verbal communication in the real world cannot occur without listening and speaking skills simultaneously in use, and written communication more often than not comes as a response to reading written stimuli, such as email exchanges or text messages. Nonetheless, for the purpose of identifying effective practice in skill teaching, we discuss each skill individually below.

Teaching listening

Listening is a particularly challenging skill to teach and often teachers, even after many years of experience, feel unequipped to teach their learners to be successful in listening comprehension assessment or exams. In addition, it is widely acknowledged that learners find listening comprehension more difficult because it often requires listening to long sections of language from an audio, spoken at near normal speed, with little to no clues about the context apart from the task title and instruction. As a result, this can become a source of demotivation. Listening is also the perfect example of what we stated previously: that more practice in the classroom does not necessarily mean learners will become more successful over time.

Listening skill practice

The distinction and the progression model detailed in the previous section can be an effective way of planning listening practice. In the early stages of language acquisition, the teacher should provide controlled input practice, i.e. practice where the source has high comprehensible input. Such practice is also often referred to as micro-listening practice. Practice tasks focus exclusively on the language being taught in the lesson, with lots of repetitions and a focus on the association between the written form of the language and its oral form, rather than comprehension. Some examples of such practice are given below.

Match-up activities

This can be exclusively in the TL, as learners are given a visual stimulus with words, chunks of language or sentences and they listen to an audio in which the language is spoken in a different order. Learners must pay attention to each audio occurrence and identify which written form to associate it with. This can be also adapted to include some low-level form of comprehension by providing the written forms in English, so learners match the oral form of the language with its meaning.

Dictation activities

Dictation tasks require learners to listen to occurrences of the language and either produce them in written form in their entirety or focus on some parts only as a gap-fill. With gap-fills, the choice of words that learners are expected to produce should be carefully considered by the teacher. There can be a focus on the new language being taught in the lesson, on words that have been previously taught (to assess prior

39

knowledge), on words with a specific sound that has been taught as a phonic, to assess learners' ability to transcribe SSC, or else on words that are deemed frequent in the language. Dictation can also be used to practise grammar: in the context of using multiple tenses, for instance, the teacher can gap the verbs to force learners to listen to how they sound and then use their knowledge of grammar to produce them accurately. The latter practice can be particularly useful in the teaching of Romance languages and also German, which often have distinct verb endings that students can find challenging to manipulate and therefore recognise in listening comprehension.

As in the previous activities, dictations can include a level of comprehension, for instance, by asking learners to simultaneously translate what they hear in English.

Popular variations of dictation activities are often used to promote learner engagement. Examples include:

- **running dictation** – a time-limited activity in which learners work in pairs and one student moves around the classroom to locate sources with a word, a chunk of language or a sentence, then memorises it and returns to their table to dictate it to a peer, who sits and transcribes.
- **delayed dictation** – this involves one person (teacher or peer) reading out loud the language and another person writing it down after a certain time, forcing short-term memory retention.

Spot-the-difference activities

In these activities learners' attention is once again on the oral form of the language and the focus is on identifying differences. This can be achieved in different ways:

- two similar audios with one distinction, which can be the use of different words or verb forms, such as different tenses or subject pronouns. Learners have to transcribe the specific difference between the two audio occurrences. Further questioning can serve as a platform for a grammar discussion or for assessing prior knowledge.
- an audio occurrence is provided alongside a transcript that contains a small number of differences, much like seven-difference picture activities found in children's books. These differences should not be random but instead be carefully planned by teachers and the focus can be on words that may sound similar, key words from the topic, frequent vocabulary or words that are part of a grammar concept.

Unjumbling the words

In these activities learners listen to an audio of a phrase, sentence or even a short text and must reproduce the language in the correct order, from a list of words given in a random order.

Many more activities can be derived from the examples above to provide initial practice of the language through high comprehensible input and therefore focused on the new language and with controlled input, where there is always a correct and incorrect answer. These activities will help cement knowledge and build learners' confidence in their listening skills before they tackle comprehension tasks. When the teacher has assessed that learners are confident with the new language, then listening comprehension should be the next step. Those tasks can continue to be carefully scaffolded to allow a smooth and safe progression, by continuing to offer relatively high comprehensible input and slowly starting to include more unfamiliar language or prior knowledge.

Cautionary note about textbook tasks

It is worth noting that in popular textbooks, listening comprehension is more commonly the norm, rather than practice as described above. We recommend that teachers carefully consider when they expose learners to textbook listening tasks and consult any accompanying teacher notes in order to get the most from them. If textbook listening comprehension tasks are introduced too early, learners may find them inaccessible and they may become a source of demotivation.

Listening comprehension

The purpose of comprehension tasks is to assess learners' ability and skill to show understanding of the language in its oral form. It can vary in complexity, depending on the nature of the task and questioning, from comprehension of straightforward messages that are clear and explicit to more detailed comprehension of nuances, sometimes from more implicit messages or from isolating parts of occurrences that are just there to distract learners' attention.

Common listening comprehension tasks can include true or false activities, 'Who said …?' statements, multiple-choice questions, gap-fill activities and questions in English or the TL. All these tasks should be practised regularly and varied to enable learners to develop specific strategies for tackling them in assessments or examinations.

Suggested methodology for listening comprehension

Meaningful practice of comprehension should involve a carefully planned scaffold around the main task. Such sequences can be used regularly to effectively teach learners to use comprehension strategies and decoding skills in the most challenging tasks, as follows:

1 **warm-up task** – this consists of testing learners' knowledge of utterances that will appear in the main task. This can be done simply by providing a list of words or chunks for learners to translate or by exploiting the transcript of the main listening task and asking learners to complete gaps (e.g. to spot differences or put it in the correct order, as described above for controlled input practice). Other useful warm-up activities often form part of the concept of listening for gist, that is, focusing on the broad, general message of the source. Activities for listening for gist include reordering paragraph headings, identifying key themes and jotting down words or phrases heard in the first listening to work out the general topic. Such warm-up tasks give learners confidence when tackling the listening comprehension main task.

2 **exploration of the main task** – the teacher presents the task or question, followed by a discussion about effective strategies to tackle the task. The purpose of this stage is for the teacher to help learners prepare before they listen to the audio, by carefully reading the instructions and questions and making brief annotations that will support their comprehension.

3 **the task itself** – this is completed under assessment conditions or supported by a slower pace audio or extra repetitions of the occurrences for additional support. If the transcript has previously been explored in the warm-up stage, it should be taken away to prevent learners from relying on it. However, it can be left as additional support for learners who find listening comprehensions challenging and who may otherwise disengage from the task as a result.

4 **recycling the listening comprehension into a reading comprehension** – at this stage the teacher should display the transcript and ask learners to complete the task again as if for the first time, by reading the transcript. The audio can be played again at the same time to cement the link between the oral and written form. Learners can be asked to note their answers again using a different colour pen, so that their responses from the listening and the reading tasks are distinct and they can compare their performance at each stage.

5 **reviewing the answers** – this is done by using the transcript. The teacher assesses learners' performance during this correction phase and invites them to identify where the answer can be found in the transcript. It is also an opportunity to assess vocabulary acquisition by questioning learners on the key words and/or to identify distractors, i.e. utterances that were meant to divert learners' attention, such as negative structures, use of different verb pronouns or tenses, use of different time expressions and other nuances.

6 **repeat and improve** – to cement the learning and strategies, the teacher can offer learners another opportunity to practise their listening skills, using a similar task and/or a similar source/transcript, with some variation. At this stage, the modelling in five stages previously explained does not need to be repeated by the teacher. Instead the learners should be encouraged to recall those stages and use them to be successful. This stage serves as a second chance for learners to show progress or for providing additional challenge in difficulty.

A sample listening sequence can be accessed through the QR code:

Finally, it is also worth noting that listening skills can be practised more frequently and outside specifically planned listening tasks. Indeed, it can be particularly useful to consider for lessons when listening is not a focus. The use of TLs by the teacher, as a way to provide some level of immersion for learners, is an effective substitute for a planned listening task. Languages teachers can use the TL when setting a task instruction, during classroom routines, to praise, reward or sanction students, or to share a cultural anecdote or story. Although this may not be a planned activity per se, it still requires the teacher to consider carefully the language to be used, so that it is accessible to learners and consistent with what they have previously been exposed to. The language must also be concise, so as not to overwhelm learners. We recommend teachers make a list of the key instructional language and structures they should use to achieve consistency and create familiarity. For the same reasons, we also suggest ensuring that the teacher's use of TL is frequent and consistent in lessons, and in the planning process you should consider when and why the TL is used or, perhaps more appropriately, when and why English is used.

Languages teachers may also want to consider exploring listening for pleasure, that is, using listening practice in enjoyable activities, away from exam or assessment tasks and perhaps more closely linked to authentic sources. Listening for pleasure aims to make learners enjoy discovering sources such as songs, TV adverts, films, announcements or even conversations between people, rather than acquiring language, but without excluding it either.

For further exploration of the teaching of listening skills, we recommend reading Conti and Smith's *Breaking the Sound Barrier* (2019), which provides meaningful and concrete ideas of how to teach listening skills effectively.

Teaching speaking

Speaking is probably what most people will associate with language learning and it can often be seen as the primary goal: we learn languages so we can communicate and exchange with others. In that regard, it may seem that knowing a language is being able to speak and therefore teaching speaking is the teacher's priority. However, speaking skills for the purpose of real-life spoken interactions cannot often be achieved before a number of cogs have been polished and placed in their intended place. Yes, it is possible to communicate very early on, from the moment a few useful phrases have been taught, but only in limited and succinct situations. More often, speaking requires vocabulary and grammatical knowledge which have been assimilated to mastery level so it is accessible quickly and responsively. It also requires knowledge of pronunciation and intonation. And although writing also serves similar communicative purposes, the latter often allows learners more time to ponder, consider and correct their language, whereas speaking is instant and requires production of language on the spot, without allowing much hesitation or many opportunities to carefully consider the choice of vocabulary and the accuracy of grammar. As a result, speaking is often seen as the ultimate skill that validates the learning, but it is also perceived as the trickiest and, as such, it often induces fear and anxiety in even the most passionate language learners.

Though the final goal is often for the learner to be able to produce the language they know in the spoken form to communicate effectively in a variety of situations, we need to acknowledge here that teaching of speaking skills takes place at various stages of learning. For this reason, we will consider the essential progression from use of speaking activities to support the learning of new language in early stages, through repetitions and controlled output activities, all the way to the practice of speaking to express oneself and communicate with others in open-ended production.

Early-stage speaking practice

When acquiring new vocabulary, best practice encourages learners to be exposed to and use new words across the four skills. At this stage, speaking activities may be aimed at reproducing pronunciation accurately, associating sounds with written words or visual aids and making connections between meaning, orthography and pronunciation.

Popular speaking activities taken from the PPP model include choral repetitions (also known as chorus drill), when learners are expected to repeat what the teacher says and which is often paired with visual stimuli so learners can associate the spoken language with a pictorial representation and/or the written word. Variations in intonation and voice can provide additional engagement for learners who might enjoy repeating words, by pretending to be quiet, sad, excited, surprised, scared or angry.

Using sentence builders, also known as substitution tables, choral repetitions have been employed effectively to model to learners how to produce longer utterances of language and, using this practice, many speaking activities have become popular among teachers and learners:

- **Mind-reader** – the teacher or another learner thinks of a sentence from the sentence builder. Other learners must attempt to guess the sentence by saying it out loud. The teacher/learner then confirms if the guess was correct or not and the next person must continue guessing by repeating the full sentence until fully accurate. The activity can also be performed in pairs.
- **Sentence thief** – each learner writes down a sentence on a piece of paper, using the sentence builder. Then the learner goes around the room to interact with their peers, trying to guess their sentences. When they do so, they must be given the written sentences and the winner is the learner who has collected the most sentences.
- **Read aloud** and **Ping-pong reading** – the teacher starts by reading from the sentence builder or from a text and pauses abruptly. The learner is

expected to take over reading out loud with a minimal pause. This can also be carried out in pairs.

Other speaking activities can use visual aids such as images to carry the meaning of the vocabulary. For best practice, it is important that images are carefully selected so they are not ambiguous or confusing to learners and their use must be consistent so that over time students can associate them with the word from memory. Below are some examples of speaking activities using visual aids:

- **Repeat if correct** – the teacher leads a choral repetition of the vocabulary, for each item, pointing at an image and doing so at a slightly fast pace. As long as the teacher says a word/phrase while pointing to the appropriate image, learners must repeat after the teacher, but as soon as the teacher says something pointing at an incorrect image, learners must remain silent.
- **Disappearing images** – the teacher displays a range of images corresponding to the new vocabulary and makes one of them disappear. The learner must identify which image disappears by saying the corresponding word/phrase out loud. Challenge can be added by using animations on a slide presentation so images move positions. This activity can also be carried out using a text from which some words disappear, requiring learners to read out loud the full sentence.

There are many more variations of these activities and others that aim to support the acquisition of new language. For further exploration, we recommended Richards (2008) and Pachler et al. (2014).

Later-stage speaking practice

Very early on in the language acquisition phase, speaking practice can be introduced meaningfully, through a skilfully designed sequence of TL questions from the teacher. During this phase, the aim of the speaking practice is to reinforce new language and its correct pronunciation and to communicate effectively by answering the teacher's questions. The type of questions and the order in which they are asked are crucial here for building confidence and competency. Here is a popular sequence of such questioning:

- **Close question** – ¿Es un museo, sí o no? (Is it a museum, yes or no? [picture of a museum is displayed on a board or flashcard]) The learner responds verbally using either 'sí' or 'no' (yes or no), thus showing they can correctly associate vocabulary with stimuli.

- **Multiple choice** – *¿Es un museo o es una tienda?* (Is it a museum or is it a shop? [picture of a museum is displayed on a board or flashcard]) The learner responds verbally by repeating the correct option, thus showing they can replicate accurate pronunciation of the correct word.
- **Open question** – *¿Qué es?* (picture of a museum is displayed on a board or flashcard). The learner responds verbally with a one-word answer ('*museo*') or a phrase ('*Es un museo*'), this time showing they can reproduce the new language without prompts.
- **Follow-up question** – *¿Te gusta el museo?* (Do you like the museum?) The learner is expected to produce the new language (in this example, places in town) in a familiar structure (here, a justified opinion). An example of an expected answer could be '*Sí, me gusta el museo porque es interesante.*'

Speaking skills should also be encouraged through meaningful practice where communication is the ultimate goal. To this effect, speaking activities can be closed- or open-ended and they can be aided by stimuli and/or instructions provided at the start. We always recommend providing ample modelling of the tasks. Success criteria are also an effective way to provide learners with clear expectations on how to complete the task. Below we review some useful communicative speaking activities.

Role-plays have been a standard form of speaking assessment for decades, designed to test how learners would cope in a replicated real-life situation in a TL country. Provided with the context of a genuine situation, either transactional or conversational, learners are expected to take part in a simulated interaction and to produce spoken language to communicate effectively with an interlocutor. Often, role-plays use visual stimuli where cues are given about the direction of the conversation/transaction, to aid learners. The stimuli can be closed-ended, meaning that the interaction is restricted to what is prescribed, or open-ended, in which case the stimuli serve as a conversation starter, but soon the interaction moves towards unpredicted elements as both speakers must respond to one another effectively. The use of props and scenarios can have a positive impact on learners' apprehension towards speaking as they take on a role.

Below are some recommended strategies for preparing students to role-play activities:

- Pair up learners and instruct them to prepare a dialogue in a specific situation. This can be aided by providing learners with certain structures, allowing a rehearsal period, offering props, etc.
- Review model answers for exam-type role-play tasks and pick out their specific features. Similarly it can be effective to review wrong answers and identify why students did not respond appropriately to the prompt.
- Encourage students to perform a role-play with peers and peer-mark them, using learner-friendly assessment grids. If learners know how to accurately assess a role-play, they will know how to answer the task effectively.

Presentations can also be a meaningful way to test learners' speaking. Learners are expected to present on a topic of their choice for a limited amount of time in front of an audience. Preparation time is often given beforehand to allow learners to consider what language they will need and to organise their ideas. Scripts or notes can be allowed to support learners who may need it. Follow-up questions from the audience or the teacher can also test learners' ability to respond spontaneously to unpredicted elements. Variations of presentation exercises include photo description, whereby learners are expected to talk about a photograph and take part in a follow-up conversation on the topic of the photo. It is worth noting that photo descriptions can be an excellent opportunity to find out about learners' passions and invite them to share with a group or the class. Photo description is also often used as another response-to-stimuli speaking task, including in assessments and examinations.

Effective strategies to support learners for presentation/photo tasks include:

- providing models of presentations and success criteria
- providing a template structure or supporting material such as sentence builders
- allowing rehearsals in pairs
- allowing learners to record their presentations at home, if they feel more comfortable doing so.

Group Talk

Group Talk is an initiative pioneered by Greg Horton in his school in the early 2000s and has been praised for its visible positive impact on engagement and motivation of learners. Group Talk is a task that provides learners with the opportunity to interact with their peers in engaging conversations, discussions or debates on topics that they are interested in and that they find relevant, by using prompts such as cards or items. Picture this: a group of four learners around a table where a selection of pictures of various hobbies has been placed. To initiate an exchange, it is up to one of them to pick a stimulus and give an opinion about it, then to ask one of their peers about their opinion, whether they agree or disagree, in turns, until all have spoken. It can be optimised by rearranging the classroom in group tables that encourage learners to face each other. It is carefully structured and modelled so all learners know what they are expected to do and how they can meet these expectations. It requires time to implement and get right so that all learners engage with group talks in a less supervised environment. Group Talks are also incremented in steps so that they are progressive and allow all learners to communicate effectively at all stages of their learning. Group Talks are a particularly effective way for teachers to assess learners' speaking skills, as they can visit tables to listen to conversations and provide instant feedback. Horton noted that this technique also had a visible impact on engagement and on learners' motivation for the subject.

Link: Group Talk (https://speakeasi.net/group-talk/)

Correction of activities

During the correction of activities, learners can be invited to share their responses in the TL. This can be aided by the use of displays or chatty mats. In the context of a true/false activity, a learner could respond using the structure 'Je pense que la phrase une c'est vrai parce que dans le texte, il/elle dit …'. Additional challenge can be included by requesting that the next person must not use the same opinion phrase of conjunction, thus practising variation in vocabulary.

Expressing views and opinions

When the visual stimuli (texts, photos, posters or videos) are being introduced, learners can be encouraged to express and justify their opinions ('À mon avis la photo est belle car il y a un beau paysage et il fait beau.'). This can be developed into a discussion or debate whereby other learners are expected to express their agreement/disagreement with their peers ('Je ne suis pas d'accord, je dirais que …'; 'Moi, je suis d'accord, je crois que …').

Classroom routines

We have previously made the point that classroom routines are an ideal opportunity for the teacher to use the TL to create a level of immersion and familiarity with the language (see 'Teaching listening', p. 43). However, classroom routines are also the perfect opportunity for learners to produce the TL orally. If routines are frequent and repetitive, learners will become more and more confident in using the TL spontaneously and it will become more and more effortless. For example:

- systematic expectations of greetings and short, informal questions ('How are you today?') at the door as the class comes in
- regular register-taking in the TL
- practising the same questions over and over
- a question that is the focus of current study or questions from previous topics, for retrieval purposes
- teaching learners the language and structures required to interact with the teacher and others in the classroom context in order to ask for equipment, collect something, get help or elicit vocabulary, for instance.

All these routines can be implemented with the support of chatty mats and displays in the initial phase and, as long as they are practised frequently, they will become automatic and spontaneous.

It is the dream of many languages teachers to have well-oiled routines that take place with little or no prompt from the teacher and gradually increase peer interactions. The key to achieving this goal also depends on the teacher:

- not responding to a callout of 'Miss/Sir' unless it is 'Señora/Señor', 'Madame/Monsieur' or 'Herr/Frau'
- not giving out vocabulary unless the learner asks 'Comment dit-on ...?', or pens and paper, unless you hear the question '¿Puedo tener un bolí/una hoja?'
- giving students a look each time they say 'Thank you' or 'Please' instead of 'Danke' or 'Bitte', which learners will quickly learn to correct promptly.

Routines can be tedious in implementation, but they are well worth the effort and time and they will always impress any teachers, languages specialists or not, if when they walk by your classroom, they hear the learners interact with you and others in the TL. For further reading on setting up TL routines and the authentic use of language in the classroom, we recommend James Stubbs's blog (https://jamesstubbs.wordpress.com).

Assessing speaking

Arranging a speaking assessment can become a real challenge for languages teachers, as too often they may require one-to-one interaction with a learner during the lesson. What other learners should do in the meantime, how much time can be spent with an individual and how to administer the assessment are all factors that can prevent languages teachers from assessing learners' speaking skills. When a formal or more official speaking assessment is needed, often teachers may be required to organise speaking days, during which they may come off their teaching duties to conduct speaking examinations and schedule each learner an allocated time to sit their assessment. We recommend this approach in the later stages of languages education, when learners are studying for a public examination, for instance, and there is a need for them to experience the process, in order to reduce the anxiety it may cause, create familiarities and receive necessary feedback on performance. However, assessing speaking skills should not be limited to this form, which is unlikely to take place regularly because of the onerous arrangements required. Below are some other recommendations for assessing speaking skills in the classroom:

- **peer assessment** – this can be particularly effective for tasks like role-plays, as each learner can be assigned a specific role. Modelling peer assessment in front of the class is essential for supporting learners in understanding how to accurately assess their peers' performance. Providing a clear structure for the speaking task, with success criteria or assessment grids and with examples, can be an effective way of implementing speaking peer assessment. However, it is worth noting that peer assessment will be more and more effective as it becomes a routine and therefore the teacher should accept that in the initial implementation, success may not be achieved as intended or across all pairs. During peer speaking assessment, it is recommended for the teacher to circulate to identify common errors, particularly errors of pronunciation, and to interrupt the activity to provide class feedback or tackle misconceptions (through whole-class pronunciation, for instance).

- **class participation** – this was perhaps more popular in the 1980s and 1990s than nowadays, but it has its benefits if executed well, as it can be done frequently and can take into consideration performance over time, rather than at just one point during the term. The teacher creates opportunities in the lesson to ask individual learners familiar or topical questions in the TL and they are expected to respond spontaneously. The register can be a useful platform for conducting such an exercise, while learners complete an independent starter activity. In this situation, rather than greeting the learner in the TL, the teacher would ask a question '*¿Qué te gusta hacer en tu tiempo libre?*', either on the topic of current or prior studies, to retrieve prior knowledge. This can also be a useful strategy to identify misconceptions and prompt learning discussions. If a class has more than 25 learners, the teacher can opt to rotate the learners across the week, so only five to ten questions are asked every lesson.

- **one-to-one assessment** – this can still be undertaken in the classroom as long as the teacher carefully considers what other learners should do in the meantime. We would recommend conducting these during longer individual, silent tasks and across several lessons, to allow all learners to be assessed. The assessment can be presented and prepared as a class first, before another task is set, and then the teacher invites the learners one at a time to the desk. The task should be succinct enough to allow the teacher to gain a snapshot of a learner's progress, while also being able to conduct it with a number of learners in one lesson. It is important to consider the place and position of the assessment, as it may be useful for the teacher to still have full view of the class to manage learning and expectations, but this can be to the detriment of providing enough privacy to less confident learners who may underperform as a result of having to carry out the task in front of the class. Increasingly, technology is offering more effective ways to practise and test speaking. Indeed, the use of computers, tablets or even video/audio recorders allows teachers to collect short performances from learners, whether in the classroom or at home. Many schools have also invested in language laboratory suites, which can be used for the purpose of speaking practice and testing.

For further exploration of teaching speaking, we recommend Richards (2008) and Pachler et al. (2014).

Teaching reading

As with the other skills, the skill of reading in a foreign language must be explicitly taught. Learners are often given a reading task from a textbook and told 'Now we are going to do a reading task. Off you go!' Students then sit quietly or in silence for 10 minutes staring at the page, perhaps making a few guesses and waiting to be told the answers at the end. For students to really benefit and learn from a reading task, we must carefully plan these activities as we would a speaking or writing task and give them enough time within the lesson.

Preparing reading activities

As with listening, use reading activities in textbooks with caution as they may include too much unknown vocabulary or not support learners in mastering the structures you need them to. Think carefully about the purpose of the activity and adapt the text and tasks. Is it exam practice? Do you want them to see a grammatical structure in action in a longer text? Are you preparing them for a piece of writing?

You will also need to consider carefully the needs of your learners. First, ensure that the text is accessible with clear fonts, text size and background. You can further differentiate reading texts by using accompanying pictures, highlighting key words or ideas and considering carefully where and to whom you circulate first when students are working on the task. Avoid giving out different versions of the text to different learners according to their learning profile. This demoralises students and limits their ambitions. Instead opt for the 'all, most, some' approach, where the task is split into three different levels of challenge: the ones that all students can and must complete, those that most will do and some that some will do. When planning for challenge it is vital that these tasks have a genuinely higher level of cognitive challenge and are not just more work. Again this is demotivating for learners working at this level who may feel they are simply being given more work and they do not see the value of completing the task.

Skills required and suggested structure

For students to access reading texts, they must have a good foundation in the vocabulary and grammar that will be used and then have some strategies to deal with the unknown language. These skills must be modelled and taught. When setting a reading task, you could go through these steps:

- **think, pair, share** – what is the task asking? Is it true/false?
- **prediction and intelligent guesses** – if the task requires open answers, look at the questions and try to predict what the answers might be. For example, if a question asks 'What does the teenager do at lunchtime at

school?', we can predict the answer might be something like chat with their friends, eat lunch in the canteen, do homework, etc.
- **read the text together as a class for gist** – this is also a fantastic opportunity for students to practise their pronunciation and fluency and to hear teacher models of excellent pronunciation and fluency.
- **red herrings, tricks and traps** – remind students that we read the text as a whole so that we do not fall into common traps. Give an example, such as when a question asks 'What is someone's favourite activity?' but the sentence before mentions two things they like before mentioning the favourite. Learners who do not read to the end of the sentence make the mistake of writing the two liked activities as they miss the favourite.
- **coping with unknown language** – reassure learners that there will always be unknown words. Encourage them to focus on what they do know by underlining or highlighting these known words and cognates.
- **give clear timings** – move learners on so they do not fixate on the one question they cannot answer and neglect to answer the others.
- **correcting the work** – when going through the answers, ask learners to explain how they reached their conclusion by giving examples from the text to justify their response. This shows you that they have truly understood the meaning.

Exploiting the text fully

Once you have spent the time preparing and adapting your reading text, you can create a number of tasks using the text to deepen learners' understanding and create further layers of challenge. Types of activities that use a text as inspiration include:

- Reduce the text to X number of sentences or a summary paragraph.
- Transform the text into a comic strip or a series of images.
- Translate the text into or out of the TL, cover the original and translate it back. Compare your answer with the original text.
- Extend the text by adding what you think might happen next or something else the narrator would do from their perspective.
- Rewrite the text using a different subject pronoun or tense.
- Prioritise the key points from the text and put them in order of importance.

Links: Steven Fawkes and using song lyrics in lessons (www.all-languages.org.uk/product/encore-still-with-a-song-in-my-scheme-of-work-by-steven-fawkes/)

Lyrics Training is a website that creates activities and games from song videos and lyrics (https://lyricstraining.com/about)

ELI Publishing has a range of magazines in English, French, Spanish, Italian, German, Russian and Mandarin for young learners at different language levels (www.elionline.com/eli-language-magazines/)

Mary Glasgow publishes magazines in English, French, Spanish and German for young learners at different language levels (https://shop.scholastic.co.uk/maryglasgowmagazines)

Resources and articles to support the teaching of reading skills from the Association for Language Learning website (www.all-languages.org.uk/)

Secondary Subject Networks: Languages (https://films.myattandco.com/programs/ssn-languages-session-1)

Teaching writing

As a productive, often more open-ended skill, writing can afford students the opportunity to personalise responses, express their ideas and opinions, narrate events, tell stories and be creative. Writing allows students to synthesise, practise and demonstrate their learning in a way that is not possible with more passive and constrained activity types often used in reading and listening comprehension or when translating. It can also give students a sense of security compared with the ephemeral skills of listening and speaking; students have more time to plan, select language, self-monitor, edit and organise their work under less immediate pressure. The fact that writing tasks lead to a concrete output also means that they provide practical and valuable assessment and feedback opportunities for the teacher, as well as hopefully a more visible sense of achievement and pride for students.

However, writing in another language is a more complex and deliberate process than writing in L1. It requires students to combine a wide range of language components and it is important for teachers to be aware of the high cognitive demands L2 writing places on most students. Students will need to understand the task and any specific assessment criteria, plan and decide what to write, recall and select appropriate vocabulary, grammar and structures, find alternatives when these are lacking, physically write their text, take care to spell using accents and punctuation accurately, contend with L1/L2 differences, organise their ideas, present appropriately, check and edit their work and respond to live feedback. With this range of attention-demanding processes involved in writing in L2, it is not surprising that some students struggle and that teachers sometimes observe a disconnect between what they feel they have taught and what students produce ('but we spent weeks on the past tense last term, why are they getting it wrong in their extended writing?'). Secondary languages teacher are likely to be familiar with some of the following scenarios when they invite their students to write in L2:

- Students groan at the introduction of an extended writing task. Writing may be perceived as a laborious undertaking or motivation and purpose may be lacking: 'Even if I go to Spain, I won't need to write anything down. I want to speak the language.'
- Students are daunted by the 'blank page' and do not know how to start the task or a particular sentence.
- Students struggle to generate sufficient content to successfully complete the task or reach suggested word counts.
- Students don't understand or misinterpret the question. They may omit a required area of content in their response or tell you what they did last weekend when they were asked to say what they are going to do next weekend.
- There is a disconnect between what students want to write and the language and grammar they know. This can cause them to become 'stuck' or produce lots of highly inaccurate writing in an attempt to write at a level beyond current knowledge and skills and translating from L1.
- Students make spelling mistakes linked to their L1 knowledge or unfamiliarity with L2 orthography, such as silent letters, phonemes linked to multiple possible graphemes and accents.
- Students translate word for word from L1 and introduce errors of word order and grammar.
- Students make repeated errors with verb conjugation and tenses, noun gender, adjectival agreement, and prepositions. This may occur even if students have seemingly demonstrated an understanding of these areas in earlier isolated grammar activities but then fail to successfully transfer knowledge.

- Student work lacks planning, organisation of ideas and internal consistency. Ideas and vocabulary may be repetitive or contradictory at a global level across a task or even at the local sentence level (e.g. 'I like my town because it's polluted and dirty').

Despite this range of possible pitfalls when writing, steps can be taken to overcome them and writing can be improved significantly through planned instruction and providing regular opportunities to practise.

Planning for writing

The first step in overcoming some of the challenges outlined is to take a planned, progressive approach towards writing in the curriculum and ensure students are sufficiently supported at each stage. Pachler et al. (2014) provide the following overview of the writing continuum, moving from least to most challenging and from closed to open tasks:

From
Copying
Targeted practice
Guided writing
Free expression
To

These stages can help inform long-term, unit and individual lesson planning, as can considering the following progression within writing:

From
Sounds
Words
Chunks
Sentences
Subordinate clauses
Short paragraphs
Longer/multi-paragraphs
Longer compositions/essays
To

It can be a useful exercise to consider long-term curriculum plans in relation to the writing continuum and progression above and reflect on how they support students in building their L2 writing over time. To build foundations, early in the curriculum there will be a greater focus on copying, rendering sounds through phonics work and targeted practice up to sentence level. Once students are able to produce short paragraphs, they can be provided with level-appropriate opportunities to gradually extend and increase the variety and complexity of their writing.

Students need sufficient opportunities to deliberately practise writing in concert with, and not to the detriment of, the other skills. Once they have had sufficient input and practice of the language and grammar they will need, they will be better placed to write successfully. Extended writing tasks are best and most logically situated towards the end of a unit of work, pulling together the previously learned content. They can be used as 'milestones' to orientate the learning for teachers and students, provide coherence through a thematic or grammatical focus and provide assessment and feedback opportunities. Below is an example of a unit of work that culminates in a pen-pal letter:

Lesson	Content	Main focus
1	Introducing musical genres and TL artists	Listening and reading – vocabulary input
2	Understanding opinions on different genres of music and artists	Reading – modelling varied opinion phrases
3	Giving opinions on different genres and artists with reasons	Speaking and writing – justification and negation
4	How and when I listen to my music	Listening and reading – adverbs of frequency, time expressions, negation
5	How to write a letter	Writing – teacher modelling and student drafting
6	Final pen-pal letter	Editing – accuracy, complexity and question formation

An additional advantage of building towards a writing task in this way means the end point can be defined and fed into pre-writing task lessons by the teacher to prime students, support motivation and give a sense of purpose, e.g.

Today we're going to read and listen to teenagers talking about their favourite music genres and artists and the reasons why they like them. Pay careful attention because this will help us to accurately share our own personal music tastes when we write our end-of-term letter to our pen pals.

This is not to suggest all forms of writing should be delayed to the end of a unit. In the earlier sequence, lessons 1, 2 and 4 could helpfully include some copying and/or writing of targeted words, sentences and short paragraphs as a way to support acquisition, allow students to begin to personalise language and prepare them for the final extended writing. This can help them get used to the sensation of writing the words and memorise language, even when the main focus is on the receptive skills.

More generally, it can also be healthy to sprinkle short bursts of low-stakes writing as part and parcel of daily lessons. The erasable nature of mini-whiteboards and using pencils or handing out scrap strips of paper instead of writing in books can help lower pressure and place more focus on the act of generating and manipulating language. Depending on students' level and familiarity with the topic, some such activities could involve:

- Writing as much as possible within a short time, e.g. 5 minutes on what you did during the holidays.
- Writing as many sentences as possible including a specific word, e.g. chocolate: I love chocolate, I hate chocolate, I eat chocolate, I don't eat chocolate, I ate chocolate, I'd like some chocolate, do you like chocolate?
- Writing with a word limit or word constraints, e.g. Write a 10-word sentence on technology. Write a 12-word sentence including the words 'buy' and 'weekend'. Write what you did yesterday without using the words 'I', 'went', 'ate' or 'played'.
- Writing all the words/nouns/verbs/phrases associated with a given topic, e.g. cinema, sport, the environment.
- Personalising and transferring language, e.g. Personalise the sentence on the board by changing/adding at least three words. Change words in this sentence so it makes sense in another topic/context ('I love my **school** because there are lots of facilities. There is a new library, a big **canteen** and lots of **laboratories** → I love my **town** because there are lots of facilities. There is a new library, a big **cinema** and lots of **restaurants**.')

- Writing a TL 'margin message' to your teacher. This can be easily set up and encouraged each lesson while other students are entering and settling. It could be initially guided with suggestions (e.g. What did you do yesterday? How are you feeling?) and more to free production. This can make books more interesting to mark and allow the teacher to respond in writing.

Scaffolding and modelling language

A key consideration in designing writing opportunities is deciding on the level of guidance or support materials provided and when these are withdrawn. Using dictionaries, writing mats, sentence builders and model texts develops important skills and helps scaffold writing. Below are some additional ways of scaffolding and modelling writing:

- **graded gapping** – the challenge of gap-fill exercises can be varied according to the stage of the learner and the teacher's desired point of focus, e.g. 'Hier soir, j'ai mangé des pâtes' (Yesterday evening I ate some pasta) could be gapped in a variety of ways and the words required to complete the sentence or the L1 translation could be provided or omitted:

  Hier soir, j'ai mang_ des pâtes.

  Hier soir, j'ai mang_ des p_te_.

  Hier soir, j'ai m _ _ _ _ des pâtes.

  Hier soir, j'ai m_____ des pâtes.

  H_ _ _ s_ _ _ _, j' _ _ m _ _ _ _ d _ _ p_ _ _ _.

  H____ s____, j'___ m_____ d__ p_____.

- **sentence starters** – these can give the initial momentum to get students started in their writing and provide structure and increase variety. They could be given in a list or sentence builder or as a template for students to complete. The following is an example of a template for last/next/usual weekend routine that by adding even a basic variety of activity verbs phrases to, students can significantly boost writing their output and confidence.

  Firstly, on Saturday morning …

  Then, in the afternoon …

  After that, in the evening …

  The next day in the morning …

  After having done that, at __ o'clock …

  Finally, in the evening …

- **structure strips** – these help combat the daunting nature of a writing question followed by many blank lines for a response. They help students step by step in structuring their responses and provide content suggestions to reduce the cognitive load and meet assessment criteria. They can be used to prompt in L1, L2 or both. A sample structure strip can be accessed through the QR code.

Modelling writing

Exposing students to ample models of the kind of language you want them to produce through listening, reading and endpoints helps prime them with expectations of the type of longer writing you want them to subsequently produce. However, not all students will automatically make this link and it can be helpful to make the process of writing more explicit through thinking aloud and co-construction of texts. This allows the teacher as the expert to model and demystify the thinking process and stages of creating an extended writing piece. This can be achieved quite simply and with minimal preparation from the front of the class with the teacher using a whiteboard or visualiser. The activity can be framed as 'Let's answer this question together using your ideas to create the best response we can.' The teacher then narrates their thought process and incorporates student contributions. Some useful questions along the way to prompt student thinking might be:

- What is the question asking us to do? What are the success criteria?
- Let's plan together, what are your initial ideas for what we might include?
- What tense(s) should we be writing in? Where might we be able to show off an additional tense? Give me an example of verbs we might use in the correct tense.
- Let's start with a basic sentence, who has a suggestion? Now we have some basic sentences, how could we link them together?
- How could we include additional detail in this sentence? Could you also tell me when/with whom/where/give an opinion or reason?

- What could we add to this sentence to make it more impressive? Could we add any 'AVOCADO' or 'ACTION' words? *(See below.)*
- Who can spot any repetition of vocabulary? What synonyms or alternative structures could we use instead to increase our variety of vocabulary?
- Where in the piece could we add an additional tense, a verb with another subject or the subjunctive?
- Now let's check our spelling/verb tenses/adjective agreement together.

Such questioning can also be used on any pre-made text or students' own work (visualisers make this extremely easy to do live in a lesson or a simple scan or photo of student work can be projected). Be mindful when using student work for peer assessment to focus on identifying strong features alongside areas for development to avoid public critiques of an individual's work.

The translate-and-fold activity accessed through the QR code demonstrates a sequence of short activities that provide model texts for students, with the aim of scaffolding towards production from memory and the recycling of key structures across topics.

Mnemonics such as 'AVOCADO' or 'ACTION' can be used to support students in improving the variety and complexity of language and serve as checklists for students. They could be printed on posters for the teacher to refer to before, during and after writing.

Adjectives (range of and avoiding common ones)	**A**djectives
Variety of verbs (tenses and subject pronouns)	**C**onjunctions
Opinions (justified)	**T**enses and time phrases
Conjunctions (range of)	**I**ntensifiers
Adverbs	**O**pinions
Description	**N**egation
Originality (idiom, exclamation, unique vocabulary)	

Audience and format

Although not always possible, giving a writing task an audience and purpose can significantly increase student engagement and improve the quality of work produced. Knowing that a pen pal will receive a letter or email or that the piece of writing will be displayed on a school website, school announcement screen, blog, corridor, classroom wall, or shared with parents at parents' evening can be a powerful motivator. Authentic pen-pal letter-exchange projects are incredibly valuable but can take a significant amount of work to establish, maintain and align with language levels, curriculum content and student numbers. However, there are various strategies and adjustments that can be made to leverage the sense of audience and purpose.

The teacher is the first and most obvious audience. Marking books, roaming the classroom to live-mark and praise or inviting students to come to the teacher's desk with their work all let students know that attention is being paid to their work. Otherwise writing could be seen as writing for writing's sake and some students might understandably think 'Why make an effort if no one will ever read what I'm writing?' Equally, some students will want to impress their teacher, achieve good scores and receive praise.

Peers are another useful and accessible audience. If students know their work may be marked by a peer, placed under a visualiser, appear in the next lesson's materials or go on a classroom display, they will be inclined to put in greater effort. An internal pen-pal letter exchange within the same school is straightforward to organise with colleagues and the curriculum content will align. This may seem artificial, but it is a much more communicative act than writing a text about yourself in your exercise book that no one might read and it gives students a concrete audience. An inspiring example of student work can be accessed through the QR code.

Tweaking the physical output format of a writing task has potential to positively impact upon engagement with writing. Some further suggestions are listed below.

- letter
- postcard
- fact file
- diary
- text message conversation
- social media profile
- social media post
- restaurant/hotel review
- email
- blog post
- cartoon or comic speech bubbles/captions
- film/TV script
- news headlines/articles
- recipes
- 'Wanted' posters
- advice posters (e.g. health, environment)
- maps/directions
- shape poems or acrostics
- greetings cards
- song lyrics.

Depending upon the class, students could be invited to create their own versions of these, including using technology. However, it is important to not let aesthetic design work and use of the technology waste valuable lesson time. One option is for the language work to be completed in lesson and the design to be worked on as homework. The simplest and most efficient approach is for the teacher to provide a hardcopy layout that students write on by hand. This helps to keep the focus on the language work, such as in the example of a text message conversation accessed through the QR code.

Teaching translation

In this section we will purposefully skip the debate over the place of translation in language education that took place for decades. Indeed, translation has come in and out of fashion over the years, but in *The Language Teacher Toolkit* Smith and Conti (2023) dedicate a full chapter to summarising the history of translation in language pedagogy, listing its pros and cons and sharing effective strategies to deploy it well in the context of secondary education. So, instead, we will accept that translation can be a valuable tool in language learning – not only because it is also often part of public examinations (GCSE since 2018, A-level) – and we will review how and at which stages it can be particularly helpful to expose students to it.

Let's start by making a distinction between the two types of translation: from the TL to English (often referred to as L2 to L1) and from English to the TL (L1 to L2). Translation from L2 to L1 is both an exercise in reading comprehension (reading for details) and an exercise in writing in one's first language to communicate/render a message as faithfully as possible. Translation from L2 to L1 can therefore be an integral part of the early stages of new language acquisition, as it helps cement new vocabulary. Starting from a very high level of comprehensible input, where all the language included is familiar to the learner and the focus of the lesson, it can become an exercise to drill new language and check for understanding. It's an effective assessment tool as there is a right or wrong answer each time, so teacher and learner can identify quickly where the knowledge gaps are. By decreasing the level of comprehensible input and increasing perhaps either prior knowledge vocabulary or less familiar vocabulary, it becomes a more challenging reading comprehension exercise for the later stages of learning, when learners have become increasingly confident with the new language and can use this new knowledge to decipher meaning through context.

It's worth noting also that while translation can be perceived as a challenging task by many learners, it can be incorporated into various activities and easily adapted by the teacher to cater for various needs without strenuous effort – for instance, spotting differences between an original text and its translation, identifying the best translation in a multiple choice, filling in the gaps, unjumbling the words and many other adaptations. In recent years, as translation has seen a little bit of a revival, it has also been used in engaging kinetic activities, such as running translation, delayed translation and puzzle dictations.

Translation from L1 to L2 can be described as a productive task, as it requires learners to produce the language they have learned in a similar way to writing but with the restriction of the choice of content to write about. Sometimes perceived as a task that removes all creativity from learners, translation can, however, play a vital role in acquisition of new language. As we have previously recommended in earlier sections, translation from L1 to L2, much like writing and speaking, should come in the later stages of learning, when learners have received ample modelling of the new language and have been able to practise it to feel confident with little or no support. Then, translation from L2 to L1 becomes an effective assessment tool because of its very nature: there is a right and wrong answer and that provides insightful feedback on the learning progress. Again, varying the amount of new language, of prior knowledge vocabulary and of unfamiliar vocabulary, required to be used in the translation, will allow the teacher to set this task earlier in the learning or towards the end of it.

The real asset of translation from L1 to L2 is its versatility and adaptability as the teacher can expertly create sentences or texts which purposefully require learners to use grammar structures and vocabulary that they want to test. It can also be scaffolded and supported, much as we described for translation from L2 to L1.

Translation from L1 to L2 can also be an effective tool to support production with less confident learners. Indeed, some learners may dread having to produce a piece of writing on a blank page or to speak spontaneously to answer a series of questions, not knowing where to start, what to include and how to structure it. Although we have mentioned that providing success criteria can help alleviate this fear, translation can also be a valuable additional support. Teachers are often expert in knowing what their learners know and what they can produce, so providing sentences to translate as a model for a writing or speaking production can be a way to show learners that they can produce language and be successful. Just providing the first sentence of each paragraph in translation might be what some learners need to continue on their own. Nonetheless, translation from L1 to L2 should not be the end goal of the learning sequence and ultimately written or spoken production without support should follow, as only then can the teacher identify if learners can walk the tightrope without a net and communicate thoughts, feelings, opinions and ideas effectively.

Teaching grammar

Grammar forms the foundation of any language and plays a crucial role in fluency and accuracy. Students are expected to work independently from memory, under time restrictions and to demonstrate what they have learned through meaningful creative production. To help students in reaching this level, grammar should be scaffolded through guided active tasks, in meaningful contexts, from simple to more complex ones, allowing them to express their thoughts effectively without support. The tools and activities listed below could be used to reach this aim.

Sentence builders

Sentence builders (SBs) are an excellent tool for teaching grammar in a communicative and structured way. They help students learn language patterns by providing them with ready-made sentence frames, allowing scaffolded practice. SBs support guided output, helping learners to produce sentences that follow TL grammar rules while fostering a deeper understanding of syntax. This method is particularly useful for reducing cognitive overload and promoting active engagement with the language.

SBs can be used to:

- recall a previous grammar rule
- introduce a new grammar rule.

Teachers should decide if they prefer to have SBs with L1 or just L2. The sample Arabic SBs accessible through the QR code below show both versions for clarification. In our experience, it is more effective to teach the vocabulary/chunks of the SB first through different activities and then share the SB in L2 only. This allows students to focus on just the TL.

Activities can take the form of:

- **1 minute think, pair, share** – students have 1 minute to work out why some words are in a certain colour, 1 minute to share their finding with a partner, and 1 minute to share this with the class.
- **Listen and spot the chunk** – the teacher reads out a sentence and students write the chunk that contains the grammar rule being discussed.
- **Delayed dictation** – the teacher reads out a sentence and students wait for 10 seconds before they write it down or repeat it orally.

- **Correct your teacher** – the teacher reads out a sentence, makes a mistake with the grammar rule being discussed and students write the correct form.

Short stories or book texts

For this activity, choose a short passage from a textbook or story. Begin by reading it and discussing its content. Then identify a specific grammar form within the passage and talk about how it's used in the sentence. Wrap up by paraphrasing or identifying the sentence. This approach to grammar discovery has been shown to enhance learners' understanding of both their native language and foreign languages.

> أسكن مع والديّ مُنى وعليّ، وهما حنونان جدّاً. ويسكن معنا أيضاً أخي غير الشقيق خالد، وهو أكبر منّي.
> أحبُّ أن أزور جَدّي عبدالله وجَدّتي سُميّة، وهما يسكنان بالقرب من بيتنا. يُعجبني أيضاً قضاء الوقت مع زوجة خالي ندى وابنتها ريم، لأنّهما تُحبّان الرسم مثلي. كما أقابل ابنة عمّي سميرة يوميّاً، وهي تريد أن تذهب إلى السوق دائماً، ولكنّي لا أحبّ التسوّق؛ فأنا أفضّل البقاء مع زوجة عمّي زينب، لأساعدها في الطبخ.
>
> عبير

1. Read the text and <u>underline</u> the present tense verbs.
2. In 1 minute write the verbs in as many sentences as possible.
3. Translate the sentences into your native language.
4. Rewrite the text by changing to the past tense or future tense. (This step is used if students have learned another tense to support them to manipulate the language and compare the differences.)

The teacher can also develop further activities to reinforce the grammar rule by creating activities such as:

1 Circle the correct present tense verb form in each sentence.

يوجد/ كان يوجد/ توجد أربعة أفراد في عائلتي.

There are/were four people in my family.

2 Arrange the words in the correct order.

اسم – يُساعدني كثيراً - عليّ - وهو - عمّي.

name - he helps me a lot - Ali - he is - my uncle

3 Find the words in the word rope.

العمّعابنعمّيكلّيومبعدالمدرسة

To practise writing and speaking, you can ask students to add further information to the end of the text or story or to personalise the story by writing their own version.

Creative projects

Teaching grammar in a foreign language can be highly effective when integrated with creative projects, such as using songs and storytelling, as they add context, emotion and memory aids to the learning process. Engaging students through music and stories makes grammar less abstract, helping learners to grasp complex structures in a meaningful way. Chapter 5 has many great tips and ideas, and below are some scaffolded activities that blend creativity with grammatical learning.

Grammar in songs: discovering patterns

1 **Introduce** – choose a song in the TL that highlights a specific grammatical structure (e.g. past tense verbs or conditional sentences). Play the song and provide the lyrics, asking students to underline or circle instances of the target structure.
2 **Discuss** – have students work in pairs to discuss the pattern and meaning of each instance, helping them deduce the rules themselves before you confirm or expand on these.
3 **Reflect** – students write a short paragraph explaining the grammatical rule they discovered.

4 **Create** – students rewrite the content using their own words, adding details that require them to use the target grammar, then redraft it to produce accurate content. Students then record and perform their song.

Story grammar hunt

1 **Introduce** – provide students with a short, simple story in the TL that includes the target grammar structure. Students read the story in groups and identify these structures.
2 **Discuss** – ask students to retell the story using a different tense or perspective (e.g. changing from past to future tense), which practises adaptation and reinforces understanding of the structures in context.
3 **Create** – start with prompts or sentence starters, then allow students to develop the story in pairs or small groups. You can also let more able students to start from scratch. Have students present their stories and, as a class, identify the grammar used, encouraging self-correction and peer feedback.

Each of these activities builds grammar skills in engaging, memorable ways, supporting both individual and group learning and making grammar acquisition more enjoyable.

Using digital technologies

Debates on technology in the classroom have moved on from simplistic pro versus anti-tech arguments and have led to the more useful questions of *when* and *how* technology can be applied in an integrated way that enhances teaching and learning.

When used effectively in language learning, technology can increase exposure to the TL and provide extensive multimodal practice opportunities, with automated feedback, both inside and outside the classroom. It has the potential to increase motivation through gamification, provide access to multimedia content and lead to innovative and creative task types. Internet access alone can help teachers provide meaning and relevance by easily bringing authentic TL and culture inside the geographically remote classroom. The digitisation of resources and emergence of artificial intelligence applications have also presented significant opportunities for reducing teacher workload.

However, if not employed in a considered way and regularly reviewed, using technology may eat into valuable teacher planning and student learning time, or take the focus away from the core aims of language learning. Time spent creating and animating presentations for every full lesson may not be teacher time well spent, when pre-planned teacher explanations, oral questioning and use of the traditional whiteboard could be more efficient and impactful. Similarly, 15 minutes spent weekly with students arriving to a different classroom and logging on to slow machines, then to only practise single-word vocabulary items for 30 minutes, would not the best use of limited languages curriculum time.

As such, it is useful to always first consider your language objectives and look at how technology can support these, rather than taking the technology as the starting point. The Education Endowment Foundation (2019) provides the following four recommendations for using technology to improve learning:

1 Consider how technology will improve teaching and learning before introducing it.
2 Technology can be used to improve the quality of explanations and modelling.
3 Technology offers ways to improve the impact of pupil practice.
4 Technology can play a role in improving assessment and feedback.

Recommendation 1 indicates that it is first incumbent upon teachers to make a careful and principled selection of the technologies that will enhance language learning and help students make progress. The TPACK framework below can be a useful tool for making more informed decisions by helping teachers and leaders to think more deeply about the interaction of any given technology with exactly what we want to teach (content knowledge) and how (pedagogical knowledge).

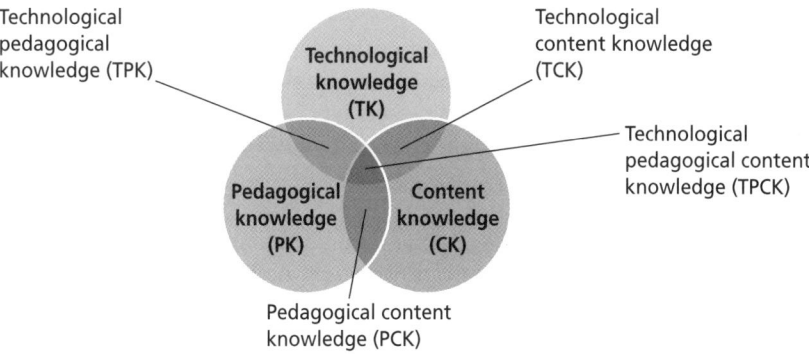

▲ Reproduced by permission of the publisher © 2012 by tpack.org (http://matt-koehler.com/tpack2/tpack-explained/)

Some digital tools are pre-authored and specifically designed for language learning, some allow a degree of authoring (teacher creation of content in a set format) and others may be generic tools that support teachers and students with text/presentation/image/video/audio production. Some prompt questions that can support your choice of a technology for language learning, particularly those that are pre-authored, are suggested below.

Technological knowledge

- Is the technology intuitive and easy to use?
- Do I as the teacher have the tech-skills to use this?
- Do my students have the tech-skills to use this?
- What is the difference between in-class supervised use and out-of-class independent use? Will students need knowledge of a particular software, sound settings, use of headphones and microphones?
- What administrator features are available (e.g. for managing student accounts, sharing any login details, creating groups, resetting passwords, setting tasks and monitoring work completed)?

Content knowledge

- Who determines the curriculum, vocabulary, grammar, structures, topics?
- Does the content align with my curriculum or qualification being taught?
- Can I create my own content (e.g. vocabulary, sentences, texts, audio, images, topics, task types)?
- Are the pitch and complexity of the content suitable for my students?
- Can students work at differentiated levels? (e.g. Is there a difficulty/year group/key stage selection? Can audio be slowed or replayed? Are there glossing facilities for unknown words, grammar explanations? Are there clues or are multiple attempts allowed?)

Pedagogical knowledge

- What does technology bring to the table in this instance? Or do I have an existing more effective or time-efficient non-tech option available? Am I using tech for tech's sake?
- Do tasks actually cause students to do the thinking I want them to? To what extent is gamification used? Is this useful gamification that motivates or a distraction from the language content?

- What range of task types are available? Do they practise the range of skills and sub-skills I want them to? Are listening and speaking tasks an option?
- Is there adequate progression beyond single-word level activities?
- Can students guess the correct answer without processing the language, access online translation tools or force click to find the right answer? Is speed prioritised over accuracy, causing students to rush?
- What feedback is provided to the student and to the teacher?

Contexts

- What are the financial and staff or student training costs in terms of money and/or time?
- What are the hardware/device/headphones/microphone/access requirements?
- Will I present front of class or do students need a device or access to a computer room?
- Consider digital equity – is there an offer for all students to access outside of lessons?

Teacher versus student use of technology

It can be useful to distinguish between the teacher's use of technology (e.g. for planning lesson materials and front-of-class teaching via a projector or interactive whiteboard) and students' individual use of technology to complete language tasks on 1:1 devices. The latter will usually be more involved and require more careful planning, tech set-up, ground rules and admin considerations. Below are some possible applications of each.

Teacher use

1. Speeding up planning and resource creation. Using a file management system such as Microsoft SharePoint or Google Drive as your team's shared area allows for sharing and retrieval of existing resources and templates. It is useful to have a bank of tried and tested activity types as templates that can be readily adapted to the class being taught. Creating reading texts, examples of grammar concepts, basic tasks and lesson planning can now be greatly facilitated with AI chatbots such as ChatGPT, Copilot and Gemini through prompts such as:

   > Create a 100-word reading comprehension text in French for GCSE foundation-tier students in England on the topic of daily routine. Ensure the text includes first- and third-person verb

conjugations and the words *cependant, parce que* and *car*. Then create eight multiple-choice comprehension questions in English. Output this as a document and include the answers.

Create ten different example sentences from the uploaded [vocabulary list/sentence builder]. Sentences 1–5 should be in Spanish and sentences 6–10 in English. Output these on a single PowerPoint slide.

2 Incorporating more up-to-date, authentic and culturally rich materials, e.g.

    a **images and videos** of locations, celebrities, film posters, book covers, foods or topical events (screenshot or image snip tools are very useful for this)

    b **virtual tours** of cities, famous sites and buildings with Google Earth, Streetview, YouTube videos or site-specific virtual 360 tours like a virtual tour of the Eiffel Tower (www.toureiffel.paris/en/news/recreation/virtual-tour-eiffel-tower)

    c live visit or screenshot websites for information-finding activities, such as 'What is currently showing in the cinema?', 'What is the current weather in …?', 'What time is it in …?', 'Where do I click to buy …?' Live webcam feeds can beam the TL countries straight into the classroom.

    d **more engaging writing contexts and format**. Instead of presenting a dialogue in plain text, sites such as TextingStory (www.textingstory.com) or iFake Text Message (www.ifaketextmessage.com) can be used to provide more relatable text message context. Rather than students writing a paragraph in their book introducing themselves, a TL social media profile template such as Facebook or Instagram could be printed for them to complete and then used for a wall display.

    e **a class playlist of TL songs**. These can be used to time activities according to the song length or as class rewards.

3 Presenting and drilling new language with the option to accompany with images and audio.

4 Planned and judicious use of animations to emphasise and give clarity to a teaching point, e.g. the sequential animation of subject pronoun + auxiliary verb + past participle for the formation of the perfect tense in French.

5   Presenting published digital course materials, grammar explanations or language activities from a range of websites (including those designed for 1:1 completion). For example, Quizlet (www.quizlet.com) can automatically generate multiple-choice tests based upon word or sentence sets of your own creation. While intended for an individual to complete on a device, these can easily be repurposed to be delivered front of class for a group to respond through mini-whiteboards or hands-up voting.

6   Supporting memorisation of language and recall by sequentially removing support from one slide to the next, using the B key to blank the screen or using tools such as Memorizer (www.memorizer.me).

7   Live-modelling the writing process and thinking out loud how to approach answering a question using an interactive whiteboard or visualiser.

8   Live-marking a sample answer to a question, highlighting strengths and weaknesses and involving students in the feedback process. It is easy to showcase student writing with a visualiser or alternatively by scanning or taking a photo and including the image in a presentation. Image-scanning tools such as the Microsoft Lens app or OneDrive's capture feature help with image quality.

9   Establishing e-pen-pal projects with schools where the language being learned is spoken. This could lead to an ongoing range of activities including individual or group e-correspondence, conference calls, creating a presentation or video introducing the students' area or school.

10 Organising students' digital classwork and homework submissions through platforms such as Microsoft Teams, OneNote, Google Classroom or SatchelOne.

Student use

1   Completing a range of exercises on language learning websites, apps, published digital course resources or digital flashcard platforms, e.g. Duolingo (www.duolingo.com), Seneca (www.senecalearning.com), Languagenut (www.languagenut.com), SentenceBuilders (www.sentencebuilders.com), Pearson Active Hub (https://activehub.pearson.com), OUP Kerboodle (www.kerboodle.com), Quizlet (www.quizlet.com).

2. Listening to and reading in the TL. Students can be signposted to suitable music, radio, audiobooks, podcasts and news, including in simplified language versions. Sites such as This is School (www.thisisschool.com) and TeachVid (www.teachvid.com) offer extensive collections of videos with subtitle options and associated activities. Lirica (www.lirica.io) and LyricsTraining (www.lyricstraining.com) offer interactive activities based around song lyrics and exercises that go beyond simply listening to the song. Duolingo Stories invite learners to read and interact with stories through comprehension exercises along the way.

3. Research projects and presentations, e.g. presenting a TL-speaking country, musician, sportsperson, historical figure, cultural event or celebration.

4. Watching TV programmes or films on streaming platforms with the subtitles of the TL enabled.

5. Students can write their own blog entries and these can be shared internally with the teacher, class or an e-twinned school.

6. Recording a video performance of a song, poem, role-play or sketch in the TL. This could be aligned with an in-school competition or external one such as the French pop video competition run by the Institut français.

7. Collaborative document production is a possibility through a shared document on Google Classroom or Microsoft Teams for Education. For example, a class or groups within a class can undertake the creation of a digital magazine on a film they are studying. Sections such as the background, plot, characters, key themes, key quotes, critical reception and personal opinions could be allocated to different students who contribute separately to produce a final product for sharing. Smaller groups could collaboratively write the for and/or against arguments of a debate topic without repeating the points already made by peers.

8. Recording speaking to support pronunciation practice, confidence building or memorisation of a presentation. This could be completed via voice notes on a mobile phone or through online tools such as Vocaroo (www.vocaroo.com) or Padlet (www.padlet.com). For an example of technology-facilitated oral homework project, see Let's Talk Homework (https://files.eric.ed.gov/fulltext/ED613976.pdf).

9 Accessing reference materials such as the online dictionary, audio dictionary and conjugation website WordReference (www.wordreference.com) (the use of which should be modelled to students first) or grammatical explanations on BBC Bitesize (www.bbc.co.uk/bitesize/subjects/zrqmhyc) or Languages Online (www.languagesonline.org.uk).

10 Interacting with an AI chatbot to simulate a TL conversation of a specific level or quizzing on a grammar concept and receiving feedback.

Connecting with language teachers and professional development

Aside from supporting students' learning, technology also provides teachers themselves with a wide range of opportunities to connect with other language professionals. Such online groups can be an excellent way to access subject news and updates, share ideas and resources, inspire and be inspired, undertake professional development, access research and save one another time. Some useful starting points are below:

- #MFLTwitterati X (formerly Twitter) group 'is a dynamic and supportive community of language teachers, departments, consultants and organisations from the UK and Ireland who like to regularly share updates, links to resources and advice on anything and everything to do with languages and language learning'. It is led by @joedale, whose YouTube channel is a treasure trove of ideas and training on the latest tools and apps to support language learning.
- Bluesky has the hashtag #MFLBluesky that connects MFL practitioners for ideas and sharing.
- Secondary MFL Matters Facebook group is 'a group for language teaching professionals in the UK. A safe haven for support, ideas and encouragement'.
- Global Innovative Language Teacher Facebook group is 'a group for all who are involved in teaching languages in primary, secondary and tertiary institutions around the world'.
- A full range of training webinars are available online through, for example, the Association for Language Learning, Linguascope and Languagenut.

CHAPTER 5
LANGUAGES BEYOND THE CLASSROOM

Embedding hinterland in the curriculum

We need to ensure that we create opportunities for students to use learned words in real-life contexts to support natural language acquisition and progression. Hinterland refers to the stories which surround a specific theme or topic. It is all about using the knowledge that has been learned and drilled during lessons in a real-life context for learners. Students recycle, transform and tailor what has been learned to reflect their personal experience, away from textbooks or other guided resources. Hinterland allows students to use language creatively and naturally, and this helps the knowledge to move into the long-term memory.

The MFL classroom explores themes and topics that can be easily related to the personal lives of culturally diverse students. For example, in the Arabic language classroom, the topic 'Food and drink' can expose students to the well-known cuisines of the Arab world, which is what students need to learn about as part of the curriculum. Asking students to use Arabic to tell the story of the cuisine in their culture is hinterland.

There are many ways to integrate the hinterland into the curriculum. These include:

- project-based learning
- virtual learning/AI
- promoting love of language learning
- putting languages on the map
- trips.

In England, national curriculum specifications for GCSE and A-level (B1 and B2 in Common European Framework of Reference for Languages (CEFR)) offer detailed guidance for teachers on which themes, topics and grammar should be covered. There are common language themes and they can offer great support to MFL teachers in different countries around the world.

This is a great opportunity for collaborative planning in the MFL department, involving the diversity of teachers across different languages, from your newly qualified to your most experienced teachers, sharing hinterland ideas that cover a topic from the curriculum.

The Pearson Edexcel, Cambridge International and AQA websites have downloadable specifications with details for languages such as Arabic, French, German and Spanish.

Links: Pearson Edexcel GCSE MFL specifications (https://qualifications.pearson.com/en/qualifications/edexcel-gcses/modern-languages-2016.html)

Cambridge IGCSE French syllabus (other languages can be searched for individually) (www.cambridgeinternational.org/programmes-and-qualifications/cambridge-igcse-french-foreign-language-0520/)

Pearson A-level MFL specifications (https://qualifications.pearson.com/en/qualifications/edexcel-a-levels/modern-languages-2016.html)

AQA GCSE and A-level specifications (www-forms.aqa.org.uk/subjects/languages)

Project-based learning

Project-based learning (PBL) can be implemented through creating and performing different projects such as:

- drama and role-plays
- songs, raps and cultural dances
- art gallery
- dual-language poems
- dual-language printed stories
- multilingual digital stories
- trips and outings.

Why PBL?

- It motivates students to write, use grammar, read, listen and speak with accurate pronunciation and fluency to deliver different messages (Dodson, 2000).
- It provides an appropriate level of cognitive challenge (Anderson and Chung, 2010).

- It supports the natural development of thinking in another language and culture.
- It promotes teamwork and collaboration.
- It builds confidence and amplifies students' voices.
- It encourages creativity.
- It develops empathy.
- It is fun!

Teaching tips

Cover the language and grammar for a topic

One of the concerns teachers could have when starting to teach languages through PBL is a lack of control over students' linguistic outcomes. Besides, teachers have topics on the scheme of work they need to cover and assess at some point. Hence, it is vital to consider in your planning and allocate enough time to teach the essential vocabulary and grammar structures required for the topic you want to cover and apply them in different contexts and with different language skills, so students can master them in reading, listening, speaking and writing activities. Students should reach a level of comprehension that enables them to confidently apply what they have learned, personalise it and integrate it into a project of their choice for presentation.

In brief:

- Plan for a topic.
- Teach the relevant vocabulary and grammar.
- Allocate enough time for mastering the new knowledge.
- Apply new knowledge in activities using the four language skills in different contexts.
- Encourage students to personalise their language outcome through a creative project.

Planning: start from the end

To ensure a positive start with PBL, it is important to share with your students what they are expected to achieve at the end of the lessons allocated to the project. For example, if your project's outcome is to act in a drama scene, share with students a recorded sample of a strong and a less effective scene from previous years and ask them to work in small groups to analyse what makes a strong drama scene and write down the success criteria for this. Ensure students focus on the four language skills as well as the drama performance. If this is your first year working with PBL, create a model sample yourself by using scenes from the internet. This motivates students and encourages them to plan what they want to achieve with high expectations.

In summary:

- Share a final outcome sample.
- Ask students to analyse a strong and a less effective sample of work.
- Encourage students to write the success criteria for a strong sample of work, including the language criteria.

Set clear instructions

One of the dangers when working with PBL is teachers could lose control of the time students need to finish their project and the class could end up spending a term on a small project. Therefore, students always need clear guidance on what is expected, step by step, with clear deadlines and outcomes at each step. This vital stage allows teachers to track students' progress, to feel reassured if the target is met at each step, and to offer support at the right time if something goes wrong.

It is important to pay attention when working with art, drama or digital storytelling projects to keep the practical development side of it outside the language lesson's time. This can be achieved by collaborating with other departments at school, by allocating extra time after school or by setting it as homework.

Remember that your aim should always be to observe language acquisition through students' drafting and redrafting of scripts (reading and writing) and by evaluating their speaking and comprehension while rehearsing for the final performance.

In brief:

- Share the timescale of the project.
- Share each lesson's outcomes in advance.
- Keep the focus on the four language skills in the lesson.
- Collaborate with other departments or allocate out-of-lesson time for the practical development of the project.
- These details can be shared with students in the first lesson of the project.

Evaluation

As with any MFL, assessing students' understanding during a lesson is crucial to being able to move on in teaching. It is also important in PBL to allow students to monitor their progress in each lesson, using the success criteria they agreed on previously, and to set themselves targets to improve. This could take the form of self-assessment, peer assessment or group assessment. Regular evaluation helps to organise students' work in groups and allows them to pause, think, reflect and set targets to correct or improve their work. This is also important for the teacher as the final project will not show the process students went through to improve their language, performance, creative or digital editing skills.

Another effective step is asking students to document the process they went through in a PowerPoint presentation (PPT). This could include photos from the brainstorming phase, notes and samples from the drafted and redrafted scripts, photos of the teamwork, resources used and the stages students went through towards the final project. Students could also include evaluation sheets that record their progress, as well as audio samples of the speaking rehearsals.

In summary:

- Ensure students have a clear understanding of the success criteria as they work towards them.
- Plan for students to evaluate their progress in each lesson.
- Encourage students to document the process on a PPT.
- Keep track of students' efforts and linguistic progress as part of the final assessment of the project.

Flexibility and expansion

One of teachers' concerns when working with PBL is that students are moving away from the topic they want them to focus on. However, remember that PBL is a great opportunity for students to link with other topics and recycle vocabulary they have learned. Hence, it is good to be flexible and encourage students to make the main project's outcome about the topic you want to cover and leave room to connect with other topics as well as personal experiences. This motivates students and gives them a sense of ownership in their work. It also engages students in making sense of the situation and encourages them to draw on similar situations in their personal life and culture.

In brief:

- Be flexible.
- Keep the focus on the main topic.
- Encourage making connections with other topics.
- Encourage recycling vocabulary.
- Allow comparison with personal likes and culture.

Examples in practice

We will follow the five 'teaching tips' listed above with some examples. It is highly recommended to embed PBL from an early stage, from Year 7 (students aged 11–12) as their time is more flexible for creative projects without the stress of exam preparation. The topics in the examples below come from UK MFL specifications and could be used across most of the specified themes:

- My personal world
- Lifestyle and wellbeing
- My neighbourhood
- Media and technology
- Studying and my future
- Travel and tourism

Example 1: 'My cuisine' project

This example is based on the online book *Yalla Arabi* (www.arabicsawa.co.uk) and the 'Critical Connection: Multilingual Digital Storytelling' project by Goldsmiths, University of London (www.goldsmithsmdst.com).

This PBL topic has been embedded within a Year 7 theme, 'My lifestyle', which covers:

Topics	Objectives
A day in my life	• Recognise types of everyday activities at specific times. • Compare your current routine with your childhood routine using the particles 'kana' and its sisters. • Explore a few Arab traditions.
Healthy lifestyle	• Discuss your and other people's lifestyles. • Talk about health issues using different 'modal' expressions. • Explore some well-known Arabic proverbs.
Eating out	• Recognise different types of food and restaurant facilities. • Talk about problems with food and restaurants, using the particles 'inna' and its sisters. • Explore Arab cuisine.
Shopping	• Speak about your shopping habits. • Describe your weekend at a shopping centre using relative pronouns. • Explore Arab traditional costumes and meet a famous Arab designer.
Traditional celebrations	• Recognise various celebrations in some Arab countries. • Describe a traditional celebration in your country. • Learn about ways to celebrate festivals in the Arab world.
Festivals	• Learn about the main types of festival in the Arab world. • Discuss advantages and disadvantages of festivals using the passive voice. • Explore famous Arab festivals.

The table above is from *Yalla Arabi*, Book 3, 'My lifestyle'.

First, the required vocabulary and grammar is covered following the scaffolded steps below:

Step	Vocabulary and grammar	Resources
1	A key vocabulary list in the TL with the English meanings is recorded for students to listen to at home as much as they need. This allows students to develop accurate pronunciation and learn the meaning of words/phrases (chunks).	A full-sized version can be accessed using the QR code.
2	Students are exposed to the key words and chunks in a sentence builder just in the TL to give practice in using them in a different context and to explore a new grammar point or revise an earlier one.	This English version of the sentence builder can be accessed using the QR code.
3	Practise the targeted chunks further through different foundation- and higher-level listening, guided speaking, reading and writing tasks.	Sample reading texts

* Note that Arabic is read from right to left.

After following these steps, students should have developed a strong foundation for the key knowledge that is required in the curriculum.

Next, the teacher shares the project plan with students in a table like the one below. This example is based on 2 hours of teaching per week. The planning followed the steps shown here:

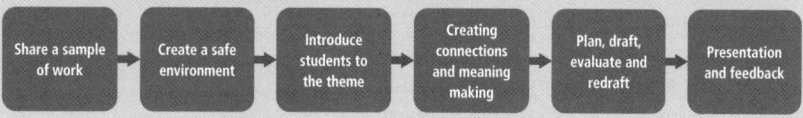

Ask students if they have further suggestions on specific points like the title or the outcome. Students should be encouraged to personalise the project from an early stage.

Project: 'The Iraqi chef'

Outcome: create a dual-language video about cooking a well-known dish from your culture

Week	Lesson	Steps	Resources
1	1	• **Share a sample of work** and ask students to watch and comment on: 1 linguistic criteria 2 performance criteria 3 digital development criteria. • **Create a safe environment** through modelling, sharing a sentence builder and success criteria. As well as sharing the video, the teacher could model the process using a video of a personal example. This helps to attract students' attention and promotes culture. Students work in groups to decide the success criteria of the three points above.	Many videos about various topics in different languages can be accessed on the 'Critical Connections' website (https://goldsmithsmdst.com/) or on YouTube. An example of success criteria can be accessed using the QR code.

Week	Lesson	Steps	Resources
		Finalise an agreed set of success criteria. • **Introduce** students to dishes from different cuisines of the TL. A possible activity could be to match photos to the corresponding name. • **Creating connections and meaning making.** Ask questions such as: • Which dish caught your attention? Why? • Which dish reminds you of a dish from your country? What is it called? Encourage students to share ideas and information.	
	2	• **Start planning** to create the video using the key stages in the film-making process (Anderson et al., n.d., p. 19). Students can work independently, in pairs or in groups depending on their level and preference. Keep an eye on the scripts as students develop them and remind them to reflect on the 'success criteria' they agreed. • Students **share the first draft** of their plan with the class. • Set **drafting the transcript** as **homework**.	**Handbook link:** Anderson et al. (n.d.) (https://goldsmithsmdst.files.wordpress.com/2014/08/critical-connections-handbook_web.pdf)

Week	Lesson	Steps	Resources
2	1	• Students share their transcripts for **feedback**. The feedback could be from peers, if their level is good enough, or from the teacher. • Students should **redraft** their scripts, **produce a final draft** and check it against the success criteria. • As homework, students **record the video with subtitles** or **collaborate with other departments** at school to support the media and digital development. Depending on your students' digital skills, decide a date for submission of the final work. This does not need to be before the next lesson; 1–2 weeks should be enough.	Students can use their mobile phones to record the video and use a video editor.
	2/final lesson	• Select videos from different levels and share them for whole-class feedback. Students should use the success criteria for commenting, reflecting on the criteria that were agreed. • To ensure all works are evaluated, share the videos on a school platform that students can access and ask them to give their feedback.	

Example 2: Interactive multilingual poetry project

This PBL sample was developed by the secondary school Herz Jesu Institut Rio di Pusteria in Italy as part of the work of the Critical Connections project at Goldsmiths, University of London. The theme covered is 'The environment'. The digital book with audio files can be accessed here:

This multilingual poetry and artwork book is a selection of poems written by 150 students aged 11–13 from Herz Jesu Institut. It was a cross-departmental collaboration, integrating artwork and poetry into a unified project conducted during art lessons, led by teacher Daniela Terragnolo, and English lessons, led by teacher Elfi Troi, assisted by Harrison Anthony Honan, over a period of 3 weeks.

Link: Herz Jesu Institut, Mühlbach, Italy (https://goldsmithsmdst.com/herz-jesu-institut-muhlbachnorth-italy/)

1. The learning objectives were identified from the beginning, then shared and agreed with students, so they had a clear vision of the expected outcomes.

Environment

Unbelievably beautiful.
Must be protected.
We don't appreciate it.
We are the cause of its destruction.
Air quality is getting worse.
The environment needs help urgently.

Acrostic poem by Maria Weger

2. Students engaged in step-by-step activities, starting with brainstorming ideas on the theme of 'Our planet' and then researching environmental issues. They familiarised themselves with different forms of English poetry and artwork in English lessons.

3. One group wrote acrostic poems in their first language (German, Italian or Ladin) with single words or short sentences. These poems were translated afterwards into English. Some students also personalised their poems by drawing pictures.

4. A second group was inspired by a bird cage that had been introduced in an art lesson. They created a picture about the future of our planet and added a short message in English and German.

5. The two groups also collated a table (see below) with key words related to 'Our planet', which helped them to translate the short poems and messages. This was also a great opportunity for the linguistically and culturally diverse students to exchange their knowledge and create a mutual respect and understanding of others.

Deutsch	Italiano	English	Ladin	Shqip	Slovenčina
Umwelt	ambiente	environment	ambient	mjedis	zivotné prostredie
Erde	terra	earth	tiera	tokë	zem
Wasser	acqua	water	ega	ujë	voda
Luft	aria	air	aria	ajër	vzduch
Planet	pianeta	planet	planet	planet	planéta
Bäume	alberi	trees	lëgne	pemet	stromy
Berge	montagne	mountains	montes	mal	hory
Tiere	animali	animals	tieres	kafshë	zvierat
Wald	bosco	woods	bosch	pyll	les
Natur	natura	nature	natöra	natyrë	príroda

6. In an art lesson, one group drew a mutation of trees in the future. Then students wrote poems in their first language (German or Italian) and translated them into English. Two students also chose to write a short poem in Polish and Spanish with the support of their families.

Ein Stamm, eine Krone, ein Stil,
Leere, der Baum und sonst nicht viel.
Die Zweige starr, der Stamm ganz kalt.
Wo ist das Leben? Wo ist der Wald?
Doch er ist stark und beugt sich nicht.
Allein, im Mondlicht.

L'albero contiene un messaggio per noi,
lui è come un eroe.
Lui è grande, è misterioso,
ma lui è anche bisognoso.
Se va avanti così,
potrebbe non esserci.

A trunk, a crown, a style,
Emptiness, the tree and not much else.
The branches rigid, the trunk all cold.
Where is the life? Where is the forest?
But it is strong and does not bend.
Alone, in the moonlight.

The tree has got a message for us,
it is like a hero.
It is great, it is mysterious,
but it is also needy.
If it goes on like this,
the tree might not be there anymore.

Picture and poem by Emma Knollseisen

A second group focused on 'elevenie' poems. These consist of 11 words of five lines with one, two, three, four and one words. Each line builds up to a final message. Another group worked on multilingual calligrams (shaped poems), English poems with translation into their first language (German or Ladin) and bi- or trilingual blackout poetry in English, German and Italian. The artwork was a result of the poem they had written.

Die Umwelt, sie braucht Hilfe.
Wir müssen was verändern.
Am besten heute,
dann freuen sich die jungen Leute.
Lasst das Auto in der Garage steh'n,
probiert mal, zu Fuß zu geh'n,
fliegt nicht nach Mazedonien
manchmal reicht auch Balkonien!
Früher war der Fisch in der Packung,
heute ist die Verpackung im Fisch.

The environment, it needs help.
We have to change something.
Preferably today,
then the young people will be happy.
Leave the car in the garage,
try walking for a change.
Don't fly to Macedonia,
sometimes even the balcony is enough!
In the past, the fish was in the package,
Today the package is in the fish.

Picture and poem by Leah Weiss
Inspired by Fridays for Future

The practical steps followed in this project were:

The aim of the book, as stated by the teacher, Elfi, is 'to give the audience an idea of the sound and melody of some of the languages that are spoken in our area and to give the learners an opportunity to convey an important message to the world through art and poetry'.

Example 3: Tourist attraction project

This example targets the 'Tourism and culture' theme, and the plan below has been used with complete beginners learning Arabic as a foreign language. Unlike in example 1, the teachers planned to start with the PBL and then move to the usual detailed language lessons. The aim is to immerse students in the culture and use the key language to attract students' attention to the theme from an early stage. This should motivate them later to learn further language. This project can be developed further after finishing the thorough language lesson and create a more detailed outcome.

Link: all the resources mentioned in the plan below, including the PPT and the worksheets, can be downloaded from the Shubbak website (www.shubbak.co.uk/learning-resource/)

Objectives
1 To explore and describe different tourist attractions (TA) in the Arab world.
2 To create personal/cultural links with these places by drawing connections using Arabic language.
3 To explore the work of the Iraqi artist Rana Abdul Jabbar.
4 To design a personal artefact/object and present it in Arabic to the class.
5 To evaluate a peer's work effectively.

Resources
1 modelling clay
2 modelling tools and base for working
3 glue
4 A3 card for colour printing and normal A4 paper
5 mini-whiteboards

Time	Steps	Skills	Resources
Lesson 1 — 10 min	**Starter** Look at the title and the images in the background (of the PPT) and discuss with your partner today's objectives. Write the objectives on mini-whiteboards. • Brief students on the objectives. • Share the PPT slides of what students are expected to have achieved at the end of the two lessons.	• Pair work (students are encouraged to discuss the points and write some ideas on a mini-whiteboard) • Reflection and self-evaluation (students listen to different feedback, reflect on what they have written and confirm the objectives in their books)	• PPT • Print the images of the 12 TA in colour on A3 card and stick them on the wall around the classroom.
10 min	• Ask students to move around the class and look at the images. Which one caught your attention or reminded you of something? It could be a similar place you have visited, a book you have read, a film you have watched, something in the image that reminded you of another event you have attended. What is the main object in the image you chose? What meaning/connection does this object carry for you? How does it make you feel?	• Creating connections and making meaning (students are encouraged to find a personal connection with one of these images)	

Time	Steps	Skills	Resources
5 min	**Matching game** • Ask students to look at the images of the 12 TA and match them to their names.	• Raising students' cultural awareness of 12 TA in the Arab world • Self-assessment *Students check their answers against those on the PPT.*	• Worksheet with missing words and key answers • Glue • PPT
20 min	• Show the first question and demonstrate how you would answer it by saying: ابة عشتار في بابل العراق. اخترت صورة بو. • Then ask each student to say their answer to someone in the class. • Go through the other three questions using the same steps as above. • Make sure to move around and listen to students while they pronounce the words and to praise them.	• Developing answers to the key questions to create a guided paragraph • Reading and writing • Developing personal and emotional connections with a place	• Flipped learning/homework *Students were asked to listen to and learn the meaning of the key expressions in a sentence builder with audio recordings of pronunciation.*
5 min	• Ask students to write their answers on the sheet.	• More able students should be encouraged to personalise their answers using a dictionary. *Less able students can use the differentiated sheet to support their reading.*	

Time	Steps	Skills	Resources
10 min	**Plenary/feedback** • Ask students to share their image and personal connections.	• Boost students' confidence • Enhance speaking and listening skills	
Homework		Practise reading the sentences you wrote and add personal information. (optional)	
Lesson 2 — 10 min	**Starter** • Share lesson objectives. Can you remember which TA we talked about last lesson? Which image caught your attention? Why?	• Recall previous knowledge	• PPT
5 min	• Play a short clip of Rand Abdul Jabbar. Watch this short clip about Rand and write notes about her. What was she doing? Why?		
25 min	Designing a personal artefact/object linked to a TA in the Arab world	• Creativity Encourage students to design an object that represents them and use it to speak about how it connects to the TA image they chose and their personal life.	• Modelling clay and tools

Time	Steps	Skills	Resources
15 min	**Presentation and evaluation** • Pick one or two students to present their work and ask the rest to use the evaluation sheet to assess the work according to the criteria and to give feedback.	Group assessment	• Evaluation sheet
5 min	**Plenary/feedback** What new things did you learn about the Arab world? Would you be interested to visit one of the TAs? Which one? Why? • Encourage students to use the mini-whiteboard to reflect on their learning.		

Link: more projects can be explored in 'Multilingual approaches through art' (https://multilingualismthroughart.files.wordpress.com/2024/01/cards_digital_final.pdf)

Putting languages on the map

Motivation is one of the key determiners in successful language learning and so for the subject to thrive it needs and benefits greatly from buy-in from students, staff, school leadership and parents/carers. This section considers some ways in which you might raise the profile of languages and promote a love of language learning among your students.

Advocating for languages with school leadership

Languages most often flourish in contexts where they are valued by leadership and they understand the benefits and needs of the subject.

Should this not be the case, some advocacy and marketing may be required and language institutions, professional associations, reports, news articles and knowledge of the provision in other successful contexts are valuable resources for making the case.

There ideally needs to be a long-term vision for languages with suitable pathways and qualifications available for students at all stages in their learning, including to A-level. This needs to be supported by adequate curriculum time for students to gain the knowledge and skills they need in order to succeed and progress to the next stage of their learning. The 2016 TSC MFL Pedagogy Review recommends ideally three lessons per week at KS3 and 10% of curriculum time at KS4. Departments need to be adequately staffed and resourced. Employing a language assistant for small-group oral work or in-class support can add a walking-talking role model for students, increasing student motivation, subject relevance and outcomes. A language assistant could be organised through the British Council, a suitable parent or someone from the local community or even an older student or native speaker within your school.

Links: Association for Language Learning, 'Why study languages?' (www.all-languages.org.uk/research-practice/why-study-languages/)

British Council, 'Language Trends 2023' (www.britishcouncil.org/sites/default/files/language_trends_england_2023.pdf)

Teaching Schools Council 'Modern Foreign Languages Pedagogy Review' (https://ncelp.org/wp-content/uploads/2020/02/MFL_Pedagogy_Review_Report_TSC_PUBLISHED_VERSION_Nov_2016_1_.pdf)

British Council, 'Employ a language assistant' (www.britishcouncil.org/school-resources/employ-language-assistant)

Curriculum time and finances are obviously finite, but there is still much that leadership can do at limited cost to support languages, such as:

- Deliver assemblies, talks and parent events in which leadership promote and explain the importance of languages and their relevance to careers.
- Provide space in school calendars and support talks, events, celebrations, clubs, competitions and trips.
- Promote community languages and accreditation in all languages.
- Make language learning visible across the school with TL signage and staff 'languages I speak/am learning' posters.

- Ensure languages feature prominently in careers curriculum and offer languages-related work experience or taster days with universities.
- Support primary transition by giving staff the time and processes that allow secondary teachers to better understand the prior language learning of their incoming cohort.

Events, celebrations, clubs and competitions

A real strength of languages as a subject is the scope and opportunity to go beyond the classroom and draw upon the culturally rich and diverse nature of our subject. This is all the more important as students are less likely to naturally encounter our subject outside the classroom. Activities that go beyond the standard curriculum bring our subject to life, are memorable and can lead to increased motivation and uptake. Some examples you may consider running are suggested below.

- **European Day of Languages** (26 September) – this annual celebration is an excellent focal point to put languages and your department on the map. A wide range of activities can be undertaken, from language promotion assemblies, guest speakers who uses languages in their career, tutor time language puzzles, 'find the teacher who speaks language X' treasure hunts, themed canteen menus and language taster sessions (run by other teachers or students). For more info and ideas see https://edl.ecml.at/
- **Cultural calendar** – identify key dates in TL-speaking countries' calendars or global days that can be brought into lesson resources or promoted more widely for awareness across the school, through tutor time and assemblies. Examples might include *La fête de la musique*, *Tag der Deutschen Einheit*, *El Día de Muertos*, International Women's Day or World Mental Health Day. Reboot Education provides an excellent free global calendar: https://education.rebootthefuture.org/calendar/
- **External competitions** – many external organisations run writing, speaking, art and singing competitions, and more for students. These might be signposted for interested students or incorporated into your curriculum and lessons. Examples include the Stephen Spender poetry translation prize, the Institut français pop video competition, the Mexican Embassy and University of Southampton's Day of the Dead competition and the Goethe-Institut's *Internationale Deutscholympiade* (IDO).
- **Spelling bees** – the Routes into Languages Foreign Language Spelling Bee competition (now run by UCML) is an excellent competition format with school, regional and national rounds in which students spell

aloud in the TL. Should you be unable to enter, you could run your own class or school-wide version. Selecting words that align with your curriculum will boost students' knowledge of relevant vocabulary and support them in class.

- **Digital clubs** – language learning platforms such as Duolingo, Linguascope, Languagenut and Education Perfect can easily be turned into an extracurricular club and run in a computer room after school to support access for all. You can also introduce competitions and prizes using leaderboards or setting up digital classes.
- **Languages ambassadors** – recruiting (and giving badges to!) students who act as your languages ambassadors gives the students a sense of pride and prestige. It can also be a way for you to identify and encourage future linguists who will pursue their study of languages longer term. Such a group can be helpful in a number of ways, e.g. teaching taster sessions to primary students, presenting to peers, supporting events/clubs and providing a forum for student voice and suggestions.
- **Film clubs** – inviting students to screenings of foreign language films can create a real buzz and support students' exposure to the TL and build their cultural capital. Encourage buy-in by allowing students to vote on the titles from a selection and just add popcorn! The charity Into Film (www.intofilm.org) offers excellent resources and guidance on running film clubs.

Trips

School trips are especially important and impactful for languages as a subject. They are often a unique opportunity for students to broaden their horizons, experience new perspectives and immerse themselves in the TL culture. They give students the chance to put their classroom learning into practice and provide a powerful demonstration of the 'why' of languages. It would be impossible to imagine PE colleagues training their students how to play football weekly for five years and never actually playing a real match, so we must afford students the opportunity to put languages into action.

Planning is everything when it comes to trips and it is useful to not just see a trip in isolation but to take a long-term view of the offer and consider the age of students and your curriculum. When deciding upon the trips it is worth carefully considering the following:

- **Audience, purpose and numbers** – why run this trip and do you have linguistic, cultural or motivational goals? Do you want to increase the motivation of a whole year group? Do you want to target a specific group of students to encourage them to pursue their language study in the future? Is it an optional trip that will run across year groups to help get the numbers required for a trip to run? The greater the number of students involved, the better, but the more challenging the trip will be to organise and run.

- **Timing** – where does the trip fall in the school calendar and how long should it be? Avoid pinch points and mock or exam periods where the likelihood of trip approval will be reduced. Consider the point the students will be at in their learning and levels of maturity. An early short trip for beginner learners will help boost subject motivation and give more relevance to future learning. An engaging trip shortly prior to subject options selection could be timed to boost uptake for languages. A longer, more independent work experience trip would be more suitable for older, more advanced learners.

- **Distance** – trips abroad have the advantage of giving a greater sense of excitement and adventure, with increased opportunities for immersion in the language and culture. However, impactful trips do not always need to be far-flung and involve significant travel. Investigate local, lower-cost options that require less organisation, such as a visit to a restaurant, cinema, language institute, business or university.

- **Language and learning** – what opportunities will students have to be exposed to and use the language? Will they have the chance to interact with native speakers or students from a partner school? Is there an organised language learning element or language lessons? Can the experience be linked to your curriculum or your curriculum to the trip through pre- and post-trip lessons (e.g. the language you will need when we go to the supermarket/restaurant/cinema/subway/meet your partner student, how to write a postcard to your family or trip review for the school website)?

- **Cost** – will the cost of the trip be prohibitive for some students? Are students and parents/carers given sufficient warning of the trip date and costs to help increase access? Can the school or students fundraise in advance? Is any funding available to subsidise costs?

- **Staffing** – do you have staff willing and available to support the organisation and running of the trip? Do you have suitably experienced and trained staff (e.g. first aiders or educational visit coordinator trained staff)? If you are struggling to staff a trip in your department, invite other staff or consider a cross-curricular visit with another department. This can lighten the organisation workload and also broaden the appeal and the experience of the trip students. Check your school's calendar and time your trip to avoid busy periods (e.g. during exams). This will minimise the impact of staff cover and increase the chances of trip approval.

The British Council's website is an excellent launchpad for schools who want to set up remote partnerships and run trips or exchanges with schools abroad. To be inspired by the international activities of some other schools, browse the case studies available in the 'Stories from the classroom' section.

For guidance on how to plan and run safe and successful trips, refer to the 'Arrange a school visit or exchange' page and make use of their school visits and exchanges toolkit. You should also refer to national guidance on running a safe educational visit. In the UK, this is provided by the Department for Education and OEAP. You can also speak to your school's educational visits coordinator for support.

Links: British Council, 'Stories from the classroom' (www.britishcouncil.org/school-resources/stories-classroom)

British Council, 'Arrange a school visit or exchange' (www.britishcouncil.org/school-resources/partner/visit-exchange)

British Council visits toolkit (www.britishcouncil.org/sites/default/files/international_visits_toolkit_2023.docx)

Department for Education 'Health and safety on educational visits' (www.gov.uk/government/publications/health-and-safety-on-educational-visits/health-and-safety-on-educational-visits)

Outdoor Education Advisers' Panel (OEAP) (https://oeapng.info/)

As mentioned, cost can be a significant barrier to running trips, but there are sources of funding and grants for students through sources such as the School Journey Association, Jack Petchey Foundation and Turing Scheme.

Links: School Journey Association (www.sjatours.org)

Jack Petchey Foundation (www.jackpetcheyfoundation.org.uk/opportunities/grant-programmes/educational-visits/)

Turing Scheme (www.turing-scheme.org.uk/funding-opportunities/schools-funding/)

Trips can take a significant amount of time and effort to organise and run, but the benefits and the memories students will take away always make them worthwhile and an essential ingredient of any languages curriculum.

Below is an example overview of a languages department's offer that gives a trip opportunity to each year group and aims to balance the practicalities and workload involved in organising trips.

Year	Trip
7	**Day trip to Christmas market in Lille.** All students. Focus on showing relevance of language learning and interactional language.
8	**Day trip to art gallery.** All students, cross-curricular project with art department. Students to describe artworks and give opinions to link with Year 8 curriculum.
9	**British Film Institute Study Day**. Morning workshop on describing short films. Afternoon screening of feature length film.
10	**1-week language school residential, Normandy.** Selected students. Subsidies available.
11	**Cinema trip.** All GCSE students. Reward trip following mock exam period. **Day trip to a university languages department.** Targeted group of 'future linguists'.
12	**5-day residential trip to Paris with school visit.** All KS5 students.
13	**Day trip to a university languages department.** All KS5 students.

BIBLIOGRAPHY

Anderson, J. and Chung, Y.-C. (2010) 'Community languages, the arts and transformative pedagogy', *Race Equality Teaching*, 28(3), pp. 16–20.

Anderson, J., Macleroy, V. and Chung, Y.-C. (n.d.) *Critical Connections: Multilingual Digital Storytelling Project Handbook for Teachers*. Goldsmiths, University of London. Available at: https://goldsmithsmdst.files.wordpress.com/2014/08/critical-connections-handbook_web.pdf

Bryfonski, L. and Mackey, A. (2023) *The Art and Science of Language Teaching*. Chapter 7 'How do I best support neurodiverse learners?'

Conti, G. (2015) 'Do teachers know how to teach grammar? Of beliefs and misgivings, perceptions and reality'. Available at: https://gianfrancoconti.com/2015/12/30/do-teachers-know-how-to-teach-grammar-of-beliefs-and-misgivings-myths-and-reality-language-teachers-and-grammar-part-2/

Conti, G. and Smith, S. (2019) *Breaking the Sound Barrier: Teaching Language Learners How to Listen*.

Connor, J. (2017) *Addressing Special Educational Needs and Disability in the Curriculum: Modern Foreign Languages*. London: Routledge.

Department for Education (2013) *Languages programmes of study: key stage 3 National curriculum in England*. Available at: www.gov.uk/government/publications/national-curriculum-in-england-languages-programmes-of-study/national-curriculum-in-england-languages-programmes-of-study

Department of Education (2023) 'GCSE French, German and Spanish subject content'. Available at: www.gov.uk/government/publications/gcse-french-german-and-spanish-subject-content (accessed 20 January 2025)

Dodson, S. (2000) 'Learning languages through drama', *Texas Papers in Foreign Language Education*, 5(1), pp. 129–141.

Education Endowment Fund (2019) 'Using digital technology to improve learning: guidance report'. Available at: https://educationendowmentfoundation.org.uk/education-evidence/guidance-reports/digital (accessed 20 January 2025)

Hawkes, R. (2019) 'Summary rationale for teaching phonics'. Available at https://resources.ldpedagogy.org/concern/parent/kd17cs85f/file_sets/sn009x76k (accessed 20 January 2025)

Johnson, M. and Mouthaan, M. (2021) 'Decolonising the curriculum: the importance of teacher training and development', Runnymede Trust.

Myatt, M. (n.d) 'Thoughts on assessment'. Available at: www.marymyatt.com/blog/thoughts-on-assessment

Ofsted (2021), Research Review Series: Languages. Available at: www.gov.uk/government/publications/curriculum-research-review-series-languages/curriculum-research-review-series-languages

Pachler, N., Evans, M., Redondo, A. and Fisher, L. (2014) *Learning to Teach Foreign Languages in the Secondary School*. 4th edn. London: Routledge.

Richards, J. (2008) *Teaching Listening and Speaking: From Theory to Practice*. Cambridge: Cambridge University Press.

Rosenshine, B. (2012) 'Principles of instruction: Research-based strategies that all teachers should know', *The Education Digest*, 78(3), pp. 30–40.

Shanks, D. (2021) 'Technology-facilitated oral homework: leveraging technology to get students speaking outside the classroom' in Beaven, T. and Rosell-Aguilar, F. (eds.) *Innovative Language Pedagogy Report*. Research-publishing.net

Smith, S. and Conti, G. (2023) *The Language Teacher Toolkit*. Piefke Trading.

Teaching Schools Council (2016) 'Modern Foreign Languages Pedagogy Review'. Available at: https://ncelp.org/wp-content/uploads/2020/02/MFL_Pedagogy_Review_Report_TSC_PUBLISHED_VERSION_Nov_2016_1_.pdf

Wiliam, D. (2018) *Creating the Schools Our Children Need*. West Palm Beach, Florida: Learning Sciences International.

Woore, R. (2022) 'What can second language acquisition research tell us about the phonics 'pillar'? *The Language Learning Journal*, 50(2), pp. 175–85. doi.org/10.1080/09571736.2022.2045683

Woore, R., Graham, S., Porter, A., Courtney, L. and Savory, C. (2018). 'Foreign Language Education: Unlocking Reading (FLEUR) – A study into the teaching of reading to beginner learners of French in secondary school'.

Zittoun, T. and Brinkmann, S. (2012) 'Learning as meaning making', in Seel, N. M. (ed.) *Encyclopedia of the Sciences of Learning*. Boston, MA: Springer. doi.org/10.1007/978-1-4419-1428-6_1851